THE
INCOMPATIBLE
PROPHECIES

CANADIAN CATALOGUING IN PUBLICATION DATA

Greenspan, Louis I., 1934-
    The Incompatible Prophecies
ISBN 0-88962-076-8 bd. ISBN 0-88962-075-X pa.
I. Russell, Bertrand Russell, 3d Earl Russell,
1872-1970. I. Title.
B1649.R94G74 192 C77-001814-9

Published by MOSAIC PRESS, Box 1032, Oakville, Ontario L6J 5E9. Printed in Canada on Canadian paper. Published with the assistance of the Ontario Arts Council and the Canada Council.

ISBN 0-88962-075-X (paper)
    0-88962-076-8 (bound)

THE INCOMPATIBLE PROPHECIES
An Essay on Science and Liberty
in the Political Writings
of Bertrand Russell

Louis Greenspan

Mosaic Press/Valley Editions
Oakville, Ontario
Canada

For my Parents

ACKNOWLEDGEMENTS

I should like to thank the following for reading the manuscript and for offering valuable suggestions and encouragement: Dr. Howard Aster, Ms Ellen Charney, Dr. George Grant, Dr. Richard Rempel, Dr. Ian Weeks and my copy editor Sandy Gage.

Anyone who works on Russell comes to depend on the assistance and editorial work of Ken Blackwell, curator of the Bertrand Russell Archives at McMaster University, and I am no exception.

I am grateful to Dame Margaret Cole for permission to quote from correspondence of G.D.H. Cole in the Russell Archives.

I owe much to my late father-in-law Harry Wolfson, with whom I discussed most of the ideas in this text, even during his fatal illness.

Finally gratitude to my wife Sheila for her support and encouragement. She did not type the manuscript because she can neither type nor spell, and my daughter Anna who, alas, still prefers Paddington the Bear.

The above are not responsible for the final result though I hope it will have enough merit to justify their efforts.

CONTENTS

Foreword   6

I   The Tension   9
II Liberty   26
III Science as Organization   45

Epilogue   68

Notes   76

FOREWORD

The essay that follows documents a disturbing problem in the social and political writings of Bertrand Russell, the problem of how freedom can be conceived in the age of technology. The discord between the two conceptions, a scientifically organized world and a free one, is sometimes so great in Russell that one could speak of a contradiction, but this term alone implies something neater than the dissonance that his writings reveal. The suspicions that were expressed in nineteenth century writers such as Dostoevsky, that liberalism, in spite of its central affirmation, conceals a subterranean tendency towards tyranny are heightened by the writings of Bertrand Russell.

As will be clear from the text, the problem that plagues anyone studying Russell's political thought and activity lies in the inconsistent choices that Russell seemed to make at various times. Writers whose political doctrines are usually considered in conflict with one another, can all seek and find authority for their differing views in the writings of Bertrand Russell. Noam Chomsky in *Freedom and Reason*[1] sees Russell as an exemplary anarchist; David Horowitz[2] has said that Russell was close to the Bolsheviks; while others find him the arch-representative of empiricism against ideologies of any kind. My interest in Russell began partially as an attempt to sort all of this out. As an undergraduate I knew Russell as one of the greatest heroes of the Cold War, defending Western civilization against the "barbarism" of Marxism. The Russell that we grew up on in those years was presented briefly in Richard Crossman's influential book, *The God that Failed*, as one of the heroic few among the intelligentsia who had the courage to resist Marxism and the Communist party in the thirties when both were such temptations. Russell's book, *Practice and Theory of Bolshevism,*[3] was a text greatly revered by those who felt that liberal civilization and the West were being threatened by totalitarianism of the East. Years later, Russell, who had all but retired from public view, was back in the headlines as a "peacenik," making pro-Soviet statements and finally championing the North Vietnamese in their struggle against the Americans. All this time, Russell's leftist works, such as *Roads to Freedom,* and *Principles of Social Reconstruction,* were issued with the intention of presenting Russell as a libertarian socialist, an exponent of socialism with a human face (such as the movement that ended so tragically in Czechoslovakia in 1968).

The first theme that I began to investigate was that of Russell's libertarianism as a response to the problems of industrial society. He wrote of these problems long before they became popular liberal causes. He wrote about ecology and the energy shortage in the 1950s[4] and about liberalism versus technocracy in the 1920s.[5] Russell, as the liberal who confronted the peculiar problems of modernity seemed to be an important theme. In examining this theme in his private and public writings, I was struck by the frequency with which he was ready to accept and even call for draconian measures, the massive use of force in order to bring about the free society. Russell as a libertarian and even an anarchist is perfectly convincing, and some of his writings are among the great documents of that persuasion. Russell as a geopolitical realist prepared to lay the foundations of a good world with the forces of a super power is equally present. I do not believe, however, that he brought these themes together convincingly at all. There is, therefore, a deep rift in his thinking, a serious crisis in the relation between liberty and the need for a scientifically organized society. It is this rift that I wish to consider in this book, in the hope that many of the other conflicts, contradictions and seeming confusions in Russell's political writing can be brought into a proper perspective.

It will, perhaps, seem strange that the key terms, "liberty", "science", "organization" and so on, are not defined more precisely in this essay. Russell, does, of course, define these terms in his writings, but the technical definitions do not give the full flavour of their usage, and their relations to one another. Strictly speaking liberty and self fulfillment or happiness have a complex relationship to one another, but in Russell's writings they all belong to the same family. Similarly science, organization and like terms tend to merge into one another, though their strict meanings would set them apart. The loose usages of these terms in this essay, though objectionable, convey the problematic nature of Russell's thought on the relationship between science and liberty.

I

THE TENSION

Though it is generally agreed that Bertrand Russell was one of the leading spokesmen of the British liberal tradition in this century, much that is in his writings and in his deeds is so peculiar to himself, and, from the point of view of most liberals, so eccentric and wrongheaded, that it often seems more appropriate to treat him as unique. Few liberals who were at one time or another associated with him, or regarded him as their spokesman, have been able to refrain from denouncing him for this or that statement or for his involvement in this or that crusade. Many of the obituaries and assessments written by admirers commend him for certain of his activities and urge us to try to forget others. Sidney Hook is by no means the only liberal who believes that "During the last ten years of his life he appeared in the public eye as a vain and crotchety figure often manipulated by others. No one knows how posterity will regard him as a social and political thinker. My guess is that whatever the judgement will be, had he not lived so long, it would have been kinder."[6] Hook is referring to Russell's activities as one of the leaders of the Campaign for Nuclear Disarmament and against the war in Vietnam. Some Russell admirers regret and often ignore his activities during the period when he was the darling of American liberalism;[7] others cherish Russell the dove and denounce Russell the hawk. Some admirers cherish Russell as an unsentimental realist and denounce Russell the utopian visionary. There is an old Jewish saying that every Jew needs two synagogues, one that he attends faithfully and another in which he refuses to set foot. For many people there are two Russells; the one that they celebrate and the one of whom they would rather not speak. All of this creates a certain disarray in Russell scholarship and makes it hazardous to attempt to establish a continuous pattern throughout his life and thought. Although in this essay I shall consider only his writings on politics and society, the problem of bringing Russell into focus still remains.

The difficulties that stand in the way of giving a clear characterization of Russell are very great. Some of these difficulties are inherent in the nature of the material; others have been bequeathed to us by Russell himself.

Of those difficulties inherent in the material the first is well-known to anyone who has the slightest acquaintance with Russell through either his autobiographies or other popular works. The problem lies simply in the sheer range of his interests and preoccupations. In the preface to the catalogue of the Russell archives, Russell wrote: "I cannot claim that my pen has been mightier or even busier than other people's swords."[8] Perhaps this was the case, but if so it was not owing to any lack of diligence on Russell's part. He produced some seventy books, thousands of articles, and wrote an average of two or three letters for every day of his life. Most of what he wrote was on the subject of politics; his pen busied itself with almost every public issue that emerged throughout the course of the century. This mass of material has inspired a number of different impressions of Russell, each of which can be documented in his writing. There was the bloodless rationalist depicted in the works of D.H. Lawrence[9] and T.S. Eliot, and the "libidinous, aphrodisiac" libertine exposed by the District Attorney of New York. There was the Russell who appeared in textbooks of contemporary philosophy, co-author pf *Principia Mathematica*, who brought philosophy and science closer to one another — a winner of the Nobel Prize, honoured by king and country. There was Russell the crusading pacifist, militant enemy of the established power, who was twice imprisoned for his actions, also by king and country. There was Russell the humanist sage addressing himself to the day-to-day problems of ordinary men, author of books such as *The Conquest of Happiness, Marriage and Morals* and *In Praise of Idleness,* forever counselling those little liberations from fear and instinctual repression, an apostle of the philosophy of follow your own impulses. But there was also the geopolitical strategist who advocated large schemes of world order, schemes that were scientific and rational, and preached that we should lay aside our inclinations and submit to necessity. Can all of this be comprehended under one single formula, or one comprehensive concept? Russell himself tells us that it cannot, that he himself sought some synthesis of the particular and the universal, a synthesis that always eluded him.[10]

Of the difficulties that Russell himself has passed on to us there are two. One concerns the genre of his writings; the other concerns his notorious changes of mind.

The difficulty about the genre lies in the fact that Russell's social and political writings are contained in books and articles, some of which are rather technical and speculative theoretical treatises, while others are barely above the level of hurried journalism composed to provide funds for himself and his school. Can his short article, "Should Socialists Smoke Cigars?" be considered as authoritative as his lectures in *Principles of Social Reconstruction?* Russell himself helped initiate a sterile debate on the question of the genre of these writings. In a sharp reply to a critic, he wrote:

With regards to *Social Reconstruction* and to some extent with my other popular books, philosophic readers, knowing that I am classified as a "philosopher", are apt to be led astray. I did not write *Social Reconstruction* in my capacity as a philosopher, I wrote it as a human being who suffered from the state of the world, wished to find some way of improving it and was anxious to speak in plain terms to others who had similar feelings. If I had never written technical books this would be obvious to everybody, and if the book is to be understood, my technical activities must be forgotten.[11]

This statement muddies the waters except for those who are convinced that philosophy is merely "technical." The plain man, who knows little of Russell's philosophy, will immediately assume that *Social Reconstruction* and other books are the writings of a philosopher, not because he has read *Principia Mathematica*, but rather because of what he reads in the so-called popular books. In the opening pages of *Social Reconstruction*, for example, Russell informs his readers that his views, if true, "seem to afford a basis for political philosophy more capable of standing erect in a time of crisis that the philosophy of traditional liberalism has shown itself to be."[12] Another major treatise, *Power: A New Social Analysis* (1938), is introduced with "I shall be concerned to prove that the fundamental concept in the social sciences is power, in the same sense in which energy is the fundamental concept in physics."[13] These statements at least give the impression that the book is a philosophical work. The genre of Russell's writing on politics is puzzling because, in spite of the fact that they are works of political philosophy, his efforts do not adhere to the strict and precise definitions of philosophy advocated in technical essays such as "On Scientific Method in Philosophy." What complicates the question is a conflict that Russell himself could not avoid. Although he had, in his work on logic and epistemology, advocated the very strict position that philosophy should abandon its ancient aspirations and imitate the rigorous procedures of the sciences, he could not, in other writings, refrain from being a philosopher in the traditional sense; a sage who dealt with first principles. This is how the public and many "old-fashioned" philosophers saw him.

Russell's notorious changes of mind present us with problems of a different order. There seems to be something in Russell that always wanted to break free of his critics and disciples alike. He appears to be waging a constant guerrilla war against his interpreters. No sooner had he been identified with a position than he abandoned it, leaving critics and disciples bereft and dismayed. Hook accused him of denouncing people for holding positions that he himself had developed. The philosopher C.E.M. Joad accused him of changing his philosophy every five years. This is not quite accurate but it is not far from the mark. Russell wrote so many memoirs, reminiscences and autobiographies that one sometimes has the impression that he wasn't himself quite certain of what road he had travelled.[14] A celebrated example of these astonishing changes of mind is the course of his activities as a pacifist. Russell first became a pacifist in the middle of the Boer War when he suddenly abandoned his hitherto vigorous support of the British imperial cause.[15] This pacifism became a consuming passion during World War I when he joined and became prominent in the resistance to the war and was associated with a coalition of Quakers and leftist revolutionaries.[16] Then suddenly in 1940 Russell disappointed many of his former associates by speaking and writing in support of the Allied war effort. After the war he was well-known as an anti-communist superhawk who advocated very tough policies against the Soviets. As soon as everyone had become accustomed to this posture, Russell once again switched to an earlier incarnation and became world famous as the sponsor of the nuclear disarmament campaign and the Vietnam War Crimes Tribunal.

Of course, each one of these decisions is defensible within the framework of the specific circumstances that called it forth. The explanation for these twists and turns that has been most acceptable to Russell and many of his admirers is that he exhibited the "empiricist temperament" in politics. Russell believed that something like the scientific temper should permeate all our political thinking:

> The essence of the liberal outlook lies not in *what* opinions are held but in *how* they are held: instead of being held dogmatically, they are held tentatively, and with a consciousness that new evidence may at any moment lead to their abandonment. This is the way in which opinions are held in science, as opposed to the way

in which they are held in theology.[17]

Thus, as evidence changes, beliefs change; hence the changes of mind. Consistent with this is the fact that Russell had made clear in his first article on pacifism that his pacifism was not absolute, that there are occasions on which wars are justified. Russell was, in his own eyes, an example of empiricism in action; the ability of an individual to become something like Locke's *tabula rasa* for each new circumstance, examining and weighing the evidence afresh and coming, if the evidence warranted, to new conclusions.

It would take us too far afield to question the theoretical and psychological possibilities of such an approach to practical questions, or even to discuss whether this is not a rather misleading picture of the way in which the scientist works in a laboratory. To be sure, Russell did exhibit and uphold many of the virtues associated with the age of scientific enlightenment — freedom of thought, toleration, criticism — but somehow the picture of Russell, the careful empiricist, forming new opinions on the basis of exhaustive studies of the evidence, does not ring true. It does not match what we find in his political writing on all levels. In an illuminating study of Russell's political writings done some years ago, H. Parris[18] has pointed out that Russell's procedure resembles more closely that of a mathematician rather than that of an empirical scientist. Parris claims, and I agree, that many of Russell's central contentions do not embody "an inductive generalization from a mass of evidence." Rather they are deductions from assumptions that were generated not by observation but from the history of liberalism. Parris gives the following examples:

These four passions, acquisitiveness, vanity, rivalry and love of power are, after the basic instincts [hunger, sex, etc.] the prime movers of all that happens in politics.[19]

Congenital human nature, as opposed to what is made of it by schools and religions, by propaganda and economic organizations, has not changed much . . . instinctively we divide mankind into friends and foes — friends towards whom we have the morality of co-operation; foes towards whom we have that of competition. . . . Always when we pass beyond the limits of the family it is the external enemy which supplies the cohesive force.[20]

There is, in addition, a psychology based on impulse which acts as the starting point for Russell's revision of the liberal view of man. This psychology is never defended on the basis of empirical findings. Parris observes that "It is hard to imagine any mass of information about the human race justifying such a conclusion."[21] The very vice that Russell sought to avoid, the imposition of principles upon reality, is far from absent in Russell's writing and, according to the memoir of his daughter, was far from absent in his child rearing.[22] Moreover, Russell was not immune to a certain dogmatism, a habit of considering his intellectual opponents as stupid or wicked.[23] This posture of the mathematician who had cooked up all the right ideas and was constantly exasperated by the fact that the world was not adhering to them was a common criticism and even caricature of Russell. J.M. Keynes says, "Bertie in particular sustained a pair of opinions ludicrously incompatible. He held that in fact human affairs were carried on after a most irrational fashion, but the remedy was quite simple and easy since all we had to do was to carry them on rationally."[24]

In view of these difficulties, there is an interpretation of Russell which seems to be gaining some adherents, the view that Russell was essentially a religious man. No doubt the author of *Why I am not a Christian* would have been appalled at this suggestion, but it is put forward by admirers of Russell such as Jager[25] and Cranston[26]. The most convincing statement of Russell religiosity is given in the excellent memoir by his daughter Katharine Tait.[27] Hers is a valuable work, a memoir that though it sometimes seethes with anger still conveys the greatness of the subject. Tait writes:

He was by temperament a profoundly religious man,

15

the sort of passionate moralist who would have been a saint in a more believing age.[28]

The impassioned rhetoric of a religious text is often evident in Russell's prose. Religious believers, Eastern and Western, seem to have recognized in him something of a sage and often treated him as a guru and visionary.

Such a view of Russell adds a new dimension to his writings on human affairs. This can be illustrated by re-examining the example mentioned above, the history of his engagement with pacifism. He became a pacifist, not only through an examination of the evidence for and against the Boer war, but also as the culmination of a mystical experience that gripped him as he witnessed the suffering of a friend:

> Suddenly the ground seemed to give way beneath me and I found myself in quite another region. Within five minutes I went through some such reflections as the following: the loneliness of the human soul in unendurable; nothing can penetrate it except the highest intensity of the sort of love that religious teachers have preached; whatever does not spring from this motive is harmful or at best useless . . . that the use of force is to be depre-cated; and that in human relations one should penetrate the core of loneliness in each person and speak to that. . . .
>
> Having been an imperialist, I became during those five minutes a pro Boer and a pacifist.[29]

Later, when the First World War broke out, he said that "I have at times been paralyzed by skepticism, at times I have been cynical, at other times indifferent, but when the war came I felt as if I heard the voice of God. I knew that it was my business to protest, however futile protest might be."[30] Katharine Tait characterizes Russell's faith as visionary: "All his life, he felt the old necessity to devote his best efforts to achieving future goals, at no matter what cost to himself, for the coming happiness of mankind meant more to him than his present pleasure."[31]

The militancy of Russell's visionary passion stares us in the face. In *Social Reconstruction* (1916) he gives a powerful description of his mission:

> Those who are to begin the regeneration of the world must face loneliness, opposition, poverty, obloquy. They must be able to live by truth and love, with a rational unconquerable hope; they must be honest and wise, fearless, and guided by a consistent purpose. A body of men and women so inspired will conquer — first the difficulties and perplexities of their individual lives, then, in time . . . the outer world. Wisdom and hope are what the world needs; and though it fights against them, it gives its respect to them in the end.
>
> When the Goths sacked Rome, St. Augustine wrote the *City of God* putting a spiritual hope in place of the material reality that had been destroyed. Through the centuries that followed, St. Augustine's hope lived and gave life, while Rome sank into a village of hovels. For us too it is necessary to create a new hope, to build up by our thought a better world than the one that is hurling itself into ruin.[32]

The elements that are combined in Russell — empiricist, visionary, philosophical sage — cannot be defined in one formula. But neither is everything as incoherent as it seems. Russell can be seen as a knight errant of nineteenth-century Whig liberalism, addressing the twentieth century. There is nothing new or surprising in this view. What is required is to show how this characterization gives a certain unity and sense to Russell's activities. What we seek is not the unity of a simple definition, but rather a dramatic unity, one that reduces the tensions in Russell's thought to some simple elements. The conflict between these simple elements, which remains central to Russell's writings, is the conflict between liberty and scientific organization. That both should enhance the other is central to the liberal creed that he inherited, but in the twentieth century Russell witnessed the possibility that they would not complement each other. These are the two themes that dominate all his social and political writings, and if one could state the problem in a provisional way it would be this: Russell was one of the great prophets of liberty in this century; nowhere is the word spoken with greater authenticity, and nowhere can the reader better catch the flavour and ancient meaning of the term. But as one of the great contributors to the advancement of logic and mathematics Russell was also a prophet of the necessity to apply science to human affairs. In our day the tension between these has become a cliche. The unity of science and freedom was at the heart of Russell's liberal faith, yet in his writing the themes sometimes menace each other and threaten to fly apart.

If we take these writings as a whole, we can look at the themes of liberty and science as two themes in one great symphony. They are related to each other, both can enrich the other, but there is often dissonance, sometimes even a frightening dissonance, between them. Is this dissonance between liberty and science, which preoccupied Russell more than any other liberal writer, resolved in his thought?

Let us consider for a moment Russell's vision of a world with complete freedom. These are to be found particularly in his books from the First World War and immediately after. It is a great paradox in Russell's writing that his sense of the great possibilities of technological civilization were most vivid during the period of his greatest despair, when European civilization was destroying itself. Some commentators dismiss Russell's early visionary works as the writings of a naive and impetuous youth, ignoring the fact that these works were not composed until he was over forty. During the war period he began to write visionary books about politics. However much he modified his views towards realism and common sense, he continued to insist that paradise was within reach. His daughter's judgement that he remained a visionary all his life is borne out in his writing. The earlier books on politics, such as *Roads to Freedom*, give a sketch of what this paradise could be like. Russell often defined freedom simply as action that is not hindered; that is, he adhered to the liberal concept of "negative freedom." In his sketches of the good society this negative freedom included much more than catalogues of the rights of individuals. Following the lead of anarchists, such as Kropotkin, he insisted that a society of abundance, in which the basic material needs of each individual could be satisfied, was now possible. Goods and services could be made available through a sophisticated technology that required less and less drudgery and labour. His own favorite proposal was a vagabond allowance — a modest sum of money given to individuals to enable them to follow their own stars and live their lives as they saw fit. In some measure his conception of freedom was derived from the example of the free aristocrats of a previous era.

This outpouring of succulent visions of mankind's future was interrupted and on occasion overwhelmed by his other vision, or rather nightmare, of what kind of world the increasing expansion of scientific organization would bring. This was the "cross in the rose," and fears about science dominate Russell's writing from the early 1920s until the end of his life.[33] These fears were generated not only by his visions of new possibilities of total war, but even by what would happen in the normal course of scientific expansion. His images are bleak and prophetic. For example, he imagined "a scientific government which, from fear of assassination, lives always in aeroplanes, except for occasional descents on the landing stages on the summit of high towers or rafts."[34]

The dualism of Russell's vision lies in the fact that he saw vagabond freedom as a possibility, and a world controlled by a deadening scientific planning and expertise as a necessity to which we must be prepared to submit. This is the message of *The Scientific Outlook*. In this book he painted a picture of the world that was so bleak that when Aldous Huxley's celebrated account of inhuman scientific utopia, *Brave New World*, was published Russell wrote his own publisher slyly suggesting that it might have been plagiarized.

Russell feared scientific organization could produce a world in which people become cogs in a machine. In a scientific world run by experts, most people will lose control over their lives; and will live as robots. "Those who have the habit of controlling powerful mechanisms and through this control have acquired power over human beings may be expected to have an imaginative outlook towards their subjects which will be completely different from that of men who depend entirely upon persuasion."[35]

Neither the freedom of vagabonds nor the tyranny of organized expertise were inevitable in Russell's view. The anarchist world that he hoped for was inconceivable without science. The average man in today's advanced industrial countries is far freer than a Chinese peasant. (Russell wrote this in the thirties.) The obvious formula is that science is a means and freedom the end. As a formula, however, this is simply an incantation. The problem is to show how a harmonious relationship between the two can be achieved. Russell saw mankind faced with two great imperatives: the need for greater liberty and individual freedom; and the need for a colossal effort of scientific organization on a global scale. Both these needs have to be met, even against the wishes of men and nations. Both were urgent, both were often advocated in the same book, such as *Prospects of Industrial Civilization*. The threat of incompatibility between the two imperatives tore Rusell to pieces. His daughter observed that "from the mountain tops of his vision of heaven he would plunge to the depths of hell."

Correspondingly, in his writings there is a complex mixture of the psychology of a stoic and the psychology of an emancipationist. The stoical element is to found mainly in his reflections on science, such as "A Free Man's Worship," where he counsels resignation before necessity. On the other hand, in *Roads to Freedom* and other books, he writes of the endless possibilities, of the paradise that lies in wait for free men. When addressing anti-scientific romantics and nostalgic sentimentalists, he insists on scientific development; when addressing tyrants and apparatchiks, he insisted on freedom. The problem was to harmonize both.

This problem was more than a problem of logic and semantics. It originated in the milieu in which Russell was reared. By the late nineteenth century when Russell was born, industrial society had been firmly established in

England and all parties had adjusted to it. As Engels remarked about the British, the aristocrats are bourgeois, the workers are bourgeois and the bourgeoisie are bourgeois. But when Russell came to maturity, the first phase of the Industrial Revolution had ended in the great economic crisis of the 1870s.[36] As he was growing up, the social and economic crisis had brought new forces such as socialism and Social Darwinism to the surface. Society was being transformed as the great alliance between science and industry that had been prophesied by Francis Bacon was being realized. The "dark satanic mills" of the first Industrial Revolution were being replaced by the new joint stock companies, the direct ancestors of the great multi-national corporations. Scientific industrialism was becoming far more prominent as a global, homogenizing force transforming men's lives and giving them new hopes and new fears. Scientific technique had been adopted by liberal technocrats and even Prussian Junkers; it was no longer a monopoly of liberalism.

The liberalism in which Russell had been reared was aristocratic and it felt itself challenged by the force of mass industrialism. The threat is very vividly addressed in John Stuart Mill's treatise *On Liberty*. The fears about a mass industrial civilization that appear in Mill became intensified in Russell's earliest writing, especially the private ones. Russell felt that industrial civilization, which his own tradition and ancestors had done so much to bring about, was now becoming a threat to liberalism. This cultural malaise was quite common in the England of the early twentieth century. The fear, as Russell once wrote to Gilbert Murray, was that utilitarianism had created a civilization of "well fed pigs."

It seems indisputable that the American working classes are far happier than ours, and that this result has been obtained by devoting all the best brains in the country to the questions of increasing output. This suggests, as many other things do, an antagonism between the democratic ideal and all other things that one cares for.[37]

The problem that permates Russell's political writing is dramatized when placed in the context of his own historical tradition. He was, as I have already stated, an heir to the British Whig tradition. This tradition is described in one of his books, *Freedom vs. Organization*. One thing which charcharacterized the Whigs, for Russell, was a passion for liberty. This was not seen to be incompatible with the precise scientific intelligence of the utilitarian reformers.

> The revolt of intelligence took the form of Philosophical Radicalism, and it was fortunate that, when reform became possible, there were men with the capacity for detail who had thought out what should be done. Owing to Bentham and his school, there was little vague declaration about the rights of man, except among the chartists; sentiment, on the whole, was left to the reactionaries.[38]

The precision and administrative capacity which Russell noted were the result of scientific training and were the weapons that would overthrow feudalism and advance freedom. Russell thought his predecessors had found the right combination and knew how science could be used as a means. But as the twentieth century wore on, it became the century not of orderly progress but of war and revolution. The harmony began to crumble. Scientific technique and its development became a menace to human freedom by the late 1890s, according to Russell. Yet he continued to be the spokesman of both, seeking the way they could be united. The depth of this problem became evident momentarily in the late forties.

In 1947 Russell proposed that the Soviet Union be threatened with atomic attack unless it agreed to the American-sponsored Baruch Plan. This episode is discussed in detail in the literature on Russell's political activities, even though Russell sometimes passed it off as an aberration in a moment of great despair. Early in the 1950s he had once again become a crusader for peace. He even attempted to deny that he had made the proposals of 1947, and threatened to sue the *New Statesman and Nation* for recalling them.[39] What is baffling about his denials is that his anti-Soviet statements were not idle threats uttered in a moment of excessive exasperation; they were repeated several times, over a period of several months. The most explicit statement was on behalf of the New Commonwealth society:

> The argument that I have been developing is as simple and inescapable as a mathematical demonstration. I will summarize it in the following propositions.
> 1. Mankind cannot long survive in the age of scientific warfare, unless great wars can be prevented.
> 2. The only way to prevent great wars is to create a single government possessing a monopoly of the more formidable weapons.
> 3. The first step in this direction — for which governments and public opinion are ready in most parts of the world — is the creation of an international authority for the control of atomic weapons.
> 4. The step has been advocated by the United States and resisted by Russia.
> 5. If Russian resistance can be overcome by diplomatic pressure, full international government may come peacefully by gradual degrees.
> 6. Diplomatic pressure is more likely to succeed if many nations join it than if it is left to the United States.
> 7. If diplomatic pressure fails, war, sooner or later, is inevitable.
> 8. If there is war, it will be less destructive if it comes soon than if it comes late, and if many nations support the United States than if few do so . . . [40]

In a address a few months later to the Royal Empire Society, Russell mesmerized his audience by saying, "I think in view of the past history of man we must take it as practically certain . . . that sooner or later there will be war."[41] The audience, veterans of every imperial conflict of the century, hardly an assemblage of pacifics, was taken aback. But in the spirit of good manners appropriate to such assemblies, a member noted that "if Lord Russell's speech had been sombre and terrifying it had also been stimulating."[42]

Most of the literature on these proposals centres on the question of whether or not Russell was advocating pre-emptive war. But, more to the point was the contention that world government had to be established in order to master science, and would in all likelihood only be established by force. These proposals were consistent with what Russell had been saying for thirty years. The development of science had made the nation state obsolete and a proper scientific ordering of human affairs was possible only within the framework of a world government. Mankind as a whole was not capable of intelligently choosing such an alternative.

This is a prominent theme in his writing from the early 1920s to the 1950s. In *Prospects of Civilization*, written in the 1920s, with Dora Russell, he wrote:

> I fear that I shall incur the displeasure of most socialists if I say that high finance seems to me, at this moment . . . the sanest and most constructive influence in the western world.[43]

By this he meant that the tendency of American finance to concentrate significant power in the hands of the United States made it *de facto* a unifier of the world. He frequently expressed the conviction that "owing to man's folly a world government will only be established by force."

In 1951, a quarter of a century later and after he had made the proposals about the Soviet Union, he wrote:

> Just as the substitution for anarchy in the Middle Ages depended upon the victory of the Royal Power, so the substitution of order for anarchy in international relations, if it comes about, will come about through the superior power of some one nation or group of nations. Only then will international democracy be possible. This view, which I have held for the last thirty years, encounters opposition from people of liberal outlook.[44]

It was after World War I and the failure of the League of Nations that Russell begins to come to these conclusions.

Industrialism has made the nation state obsolete, but the chief social and political unit in the world was the nation state. Its existence was a permanent source of aggression and hostility. It would have been better for the nation state to come to an end voluntarily but it would not die, so it must be brought to an end by force. Through the nation state, science, which has the potential for becoming a force for good, has become a force for evil. Since the time of Galileo, says Russell, the nation state's chief interest in science has been war. The leisure that science has given man from soul-destroying labour has been taken up in the pursuit of war. The only remedy to this situation is a world authority whose power will make war futile.

The liberal faith is, if anything, the proclamation of the unity of freedom and reason, the conviction that a scientific ordering of human affairs is compatible with liberty. Russell's place in the history of liberalism is among the first generation of liberals who feared that this might not be the case. They feared that something had changed. The struggle to articulate what had changed is the key to Russell's political thought. It is clear that there is a great disturbance in his outlook. On the one hand, mankind is on the brink of achieving utopia; on the other hand, the very conditions of scientific industrialism have made global order imposed from above an urgent necessity. Thus Russell is advocating something like a programme of dragging the world to freedom through force. These themes, liberty and science, are more fundamental to his thought than the switches between liberalism and socialism that occur in his writing. In what follows, I shall give a more detailed account of Russell's view of liberty; how he revised the view that he had inherited to meet contemporary conditions. I shall then sketch his views on science and how he thought that scientific organization would be fulfilled.

In Russell, we have something resembling a tragic hero of the liberal tradition of the Whig aristocrats. He was one of the great spokesmen of the scientific outlook who found himself, at the end of his life, desperately concocting schemes to save mankind from the products of science.

25

II

LIBERTY

The relationship between liberty and scientific organization is still an unresolved problem. Science and technology can be viewed as the indispensible means to the free society, but it can also be seen as a menace to it. Industrial societies are struggling to resolve this paradox, striving to arrive at a point at which science is the means and freedom is the end.

Karl Marx, in *The Grundrisse*, heaped scorn on those liberals who presented the "free individual," the Robinson Crusoe, as the product of a pre-technological arcadia. According to Marx, the "free individual" is the product of a complex social structure, with laws, industrial organizations, and the division of labour.[45] Russell supported this claim and, like Marx, he also became aware of something else — the way freedom and organization are becoming incompatible. What makes his writings, for all their brilliance, wit and genuine wisdom, so unsatisfying in the end is that Russell never succeeds in resolving this incompatibility. In his writings, the concept of organization retains the two connotations that it is both the means to freedom and its antithesis. The synthesis between science and liberty which often seems so evident to Russell is never really resolved in the body of his works. To show this it is best to treat science and freedom as two separate themes in Russell's writing, two separate concepts that lead to two separate results. In this section I shall discuss the free society; that is, the end to be achieved. In the next I shall examine Russell's concept of science and scientific organization; that is, how Russell attempted to develop a concept of society richer than the one that was fundamental to the liberalism he had inherited.

The tensions in Russell's relationship to liberalism became evident to many in the late 1960s. During this period, the West experienced a mixture of political unrest and cultural revolution, originating to a large extent amongst university youth. The New Left, as this movement was known, regarded post-war liberalism as its chief enemy and, in its political propaganda, liberal, bureaucrat, and technocrat were synonymous. Many liberals were shocked to find that the social order they had brought into being was under attack from its very heart, the university. More shocking still was to see that among the passing parade of gurus, guerrillas and folk heroes who inspired the young, was none other than Bertrand Russell. It says something about liberalism and something about the New Left that a whole generation which had taken to the streets with the slogans that liberalism meant bureaucratic oppression, and that everyone over thirty was irrelevant, was nonetheless prepared to march behind the banners of the ninety-year-old godson of John Stuart Mill.[46]

For anyone who has read Russell's major political writings, especially those published during the period of the First World War, his alliance with the New Left was not mysterious. The various ideals and slogans of the '60s had been anticipated in Russell's theories. "Participatory democracy," "decentralizing society," even "make love not war" could have easily been the titles of a number of Russell's books and articles. The New Left, with its libertarian socialism, was in significant respects closer to Russell's ideal of the good society than the more orthodox liberal technocrats.

In speaking of liberalism in general it is customary to make a distinction between its classical and contemporary forms. Classical liberalism is associated with the theories of

John Locke and Adam Smith, the concepts of the free self-interested individual, *laissez-faire* economics, and the diminution of the power of the state through a system of checks and balances. Contemporary liberalism, which the New Left specifically opposed, does not have any theoreticians of great stature except perhaps Lord Keynes; it regards itself as more pragmatic and less tied to theories. This liberalism operates with a broad concept of social welfare and the welfare state, and is prepared to accept enormous increases in state power in order to counter the power of great corporations. The central propositions that contemporary liberalism follows can be formulated as: the accumulation of power, as well as the curbing of the power of individuals, is justifiable so long as this leads to a general increase in the quantity of freedom in society. This distinction between classical and new liberalism is important if we are to understand Russell's relationship to liberalism, for he was often accused of being an adherent of the older form who was unable to accept the new. I shall indicate later on in what sense this charge has substance. For now it is important to recall that this new liberalism, which came to the United States and Canada in the 1930s, had come to Britain in the 1880s and 1890s. Russell belonged to the radical wing of the new movement and supported the break with the old liberalism in his first published book, *German Social Democracy*. Until the First World War, Russell was a liberal radical and supported the programme of reforms associated with Lloyd George. When he broke with liberalism in 1914 Russell was breaking with the kind of liberalism that we now associate with Roosevelt and Mackenzie King.

In the last chapter I mentioned that Russell was converted to pacifism during the Boer War and was disillusioned with the technological society that had appeared in Edwardian England. His opposition to American liberalism's prosecution of the war in Vietnam and the direction that American society was taking must have come to him as something of a *déjà vu* experience. Russell's disenchantment with liberalism had come much earlier, when a reforming liberal government led England into the First World War.

From Russell's point of view, the First World War was the supreme disaster of modern times, an event that set off a hideous chain of tragedies that, in his old age, he feared would lead to ultimate nuclear disaster. Russell could not forget it was a Liberal government that had enthusiastically carried England into this catastrophe. One of the foundations of this liberal faith, the optimism, the belief in the inevitability of orderly progress, died in Russell in August of 1914. He wrote later, "my life before 1914 and my life after 1914 were as sharply divided as Faust's before and after he met Mephistopheles."[47]

Russell became an alienated liberal, one who was out of step with, even hostile to, the progress of this creed in the twentieth century. Certain developments — the growth of the welfare state, the loosening of controls on personal, especially sexual, ethics — met with his approval, but on the whole Russell was alienated from the present in which he lived. His theories are a complex blend of the heroic individualism of the nineteenth century and a future-oriented socialism.

Russell often said that he preferred the company of the wind, the stars and the sea to anything human. He very often preferred the company of the past. In a mock obituary he wrote in 1936, he described himself as one whose

> life, for all its waywardness, had a certain anachronistic consistency, reminiscent of that of the aristocratic rebels of the early nineteenth century . . . politically during his last years he was as isolated as Milton after the Restoration. He was the last survivor of a dead epoch.[48]

Russell's allegiance to the past is vividly expressed in a correspondence with Gilbert Muray which lasted throughout the latter's life. Murray was a famous classicist and translator of Greek tragedies into English, but he also represented the traditional *noblesse oblige* of the Whig aristocracy. According to Toynbee, Murray adhered to that liberalism which helped the little man but could not conceive of the little man helping himself.[49]

Russell's correspondence with Murray began in 1900, and throughout it we can see how Russell remained rooted to the aristocracy of the nineteenth century. Once, hearing a radical friend praising a charwoman, he wrote:

I had heard so much about his balanced judgement that I was surprised to find him a fanatic. He is too democratic for me. He said his charwoman was more in contact with real things than anyone he knew. But what can a charwoman know of the spirits of great men, or the record of fallen empires, or the haunting vision of art and reason.[50]

Something of this remains in the correspondence until Murray's death in 1957. As late as the 1940s when Russell, after a long political battle, was prevented from taking a post at the City College of New York, he wrote Murray:

It is not growing fanaticism but growing democracy that causes my troubles. Did you ever read the life of Averroes? He was protected by the kings but hated by the mob which was fanatical. . . . Free thought has always been the perquisite of aristocracy.[51]

His most comprehensive discussion of Victorian liberalism is in sections of his book, *Freedom and Organization*. Here he discusses in some detail the work of the utilitarians, Bentham, Mill and even Cobden. Russell had, by the time he had written this book, rejected their liberalism and no longer regarded it as adequate to the problems of the twentieth century. But his criticism was tempered by more than a generous sprinkling of praise. His assessment of nineteenth-century liberalism is filled with ambivalence. Though fundamentally critical, Russell could not help but record his admiration and respect.

He began his assessment by lampooning them in a number of vintage Russellisms:

They were a curious set of men, rather uninteresting, quite without what is normally called vision . . . arguing carefully from premises which are largely false to conclusions which were in harmony with the interests of the Middle Classes.[52]

And:

The intellectual conviction that pleasure is the sole good, together with a temperamental incapacity for experiencing it, was characteristic of the utilitarians.[53]

With such introductory passages, the reader would quite naturally expect the rest to be a hatchet job on his utilitarian predecessors. Instead, Russell felt moved to defend them. In chapter after chapter he defends Bentham, the concept of utility, Cobden's free trade, and even their egoistic psychology.

Russell's often expressed hostility towards the Victorian era was based on his hatred of its sexual puritanism. In *Freedom vs. Organization* he defended even that, claiming that it was a product of the Victorians' reverence for science. Victorian "self-restraint" was based not on the teaching of St. Paul but on the evidence that Malthus had presented in his warnings about the danger of over-population. It followed from Malthus's discoveries that the rational man was compelled to live a life of self-restraint:

Owing largely to Malthus, British philosophic radicalism, unlike the radicalism of all other ages and countries, laid more stress on prudence than on any other virtue.[54]

Finally, what seemed to begin as a criticism of Victorian radicalism ended as a favourable comparison with the present age:

They were learned men and the authors of difficult books aimed solely at appealing to men's reason, and yet they were successful. In almost all important respects the course of British politics was such as they advocated. In the Victorian era the victory of reason surprised no one. In our own lunatic period it reads like the myth of a golden age.[55]

Russell was famous as a sceptic and nay-sayer. He opposed the First War, was sceptical of the Bolshevik Revolution, and the New Deal, and finally opposed the war in Vietnam. There was, however, one group of whom he spoke with unmixed admiration — the pre-industrial mandarins of pre-revolutionary China. They exemplified for him the virtues of Victorian liberalism:

When I went to China, I went to teach, but every day that I stayed I thought less of what I had to teach them and more of what I had to learn from them. I think of the tolerance of the Chinese is in excess of anything that Europeans can imagine from their experience at home.[56]

His portrait of the Confucian mandarins and the manner in which he contrasted them with the industrial lords of the West suggests the seriousness of Russell's alienation from post-World War I society. According to him, the mandarins were reared in a religion that emphasized ethics and was free from theological dogma. They mastered the arts of life and were therefore not hypnotized by the mad struggle for progress. Russell believed the mandarins had the capacity for absorbing modern technology and realizing the possibilities for a humane society that were being frittered away in the West.

For all this nostalgia, however, he did not believe that either Confucianism or Victorian liberalism was the answer to the pressing problems of the moment. No matter how much Russell admired both old systems, the present had to be addressed by a political philosophy that was entirely new.

The past provides a certain clue to this new philosophy. Russell had renounced classical liberalism in favour of new liberalism in the 1890s, and replaced this by guild socialism during World War I. He still looked upon the older liberalism with some admiration, so that guild socialism's strength was never as great as the liberalism with which he had begun.

The starting point of Russell's political philosophy was the conviction that industrial society under capitalism is a prison that breeds sentimentalism, unhappiness and boredom. The inhabitants of this society yearn for war as a liberating experience. This conviction came to Russell in one of his revelatory experiences on the night that the First World War was declared.

I spent the evening [of August 4] walking round the streets, especially in . . . Trafalgar Square, noticing cheering crowds and making myself sensitive to the emotions of passersby. During this and the following days I discovered to my amazement that average men and women were delighted at the prospect of war. I had fondly imagined, what most pacifists contended, that wars were forced upon a reluctant population by despotic and Machiavellian governments.[57]

It was the desire for war that shocked and fascinated Russell. What, he asked, was it in the structure of society that created that desire? Clearly a liberalism that was based on the concept of self-interest was refuted by this wholesale self-destructiveness. The frightening possibilities that this yearning for escape had brought about came home to him in the thirties as he observed the rise of fascism. He wrote:

Consider the huge population that sleeps in suburbs and works in great cities. Coming into London by train, one passes through great regions of small villas, inhabited by families which feel no solidarity with the working class; the man of the family has no part in local affairs. Since he is absent all day, submitting to the orders of his employers, his only outlet for initiative is the cultivation of his back garden at the weekend. Politically he is envious of all that is done for the working classes but, though he feels poor, snobbery prevents him from adopting the methods of socialism and trade unionism. His suburb

33

may be as populous as many a famous city of antiquity. But its collective life is barren, and he has no time to be interested in it. To such a man if he has enough spirit for discontent, a fascist movement may well appear as a deliverance.[58]

These observations give a strong indication of what Russell believed had gone wrong with industrialism. What was needed was not only hope for the oppressed, but hope for the repressed. Society, conceived as a leveller, a creator of the banal mass man, had to give way to a society that was liberated. Russell's judgement of modern society echoed that of the great liberal aristocrats, de Tocqueville, Burckhardt, and Ortega y Gasset who dreamed of a liberty resembling that of the ancient Greek polis.

Russell, however, went further than they did in proposing that modern industrial society could be redesigned and the stifling world of mass man could be converted into an association of free individuals.

A crucial part of his new political philosophy was the idea that capitalism had outlived its historical usefulness and had to be replaced. The recent evolution of capitalism into a system of giant corporations meant that the original alliance between liberalism and capitalism was outmoded. Giant corporations were accumulations of power that owned society and made political freedoms impotent. The traditional liberalism, in Russell's view, presupposed a society of small landowners and artisans; that is, a society of Robinson Crusoes. The ideas of Locke and Adam Smith could not accommodate the new corporations.

In saying that capitalism had become inimical to freedom, Russell did not mean that capitalism could not solve the problems of poverty and unemployment. He believed that it could. Rather, he was certain that capitalism could not build a good society, for under the new corporations capitalism had created a new form of illegitimate authority. Under capitalism, he argued, individuals who own corporations exercise disproportionate power over those whom they employ, and over society in general.

Those who are not capitalists have, almost always, very little choice as to their activities once they have selected a trade or profession. They are not part of the power that moves the mechanism, but only a passive portion of the machinery.[59]

In Russell's view the capitalist system had subverted political democracy. The democratic ideal of an equal distribution of power had been made a farce, as had the liberal ideal of the free autonomous individual.

Russell rejected the traditional *laissez-faire* liberal solution of limiting the size and power of corporations so that they would be competitive. On the other hand, he agreed with the socialists that they should be nationalized. On the other hand, he disagreed with the proposals that they be turned over to a centralized state. State socialism represented another potential for tyranny that equalled and, under Stalin, surpassed the tyranny of corporations in private hands. In Russell's view, the central error of Marxism was that it had derived political power from economic power. In his most ambitious treatise on politics, *Power*, he maintained that the two forms of power, political and economic, should be treated separately. Whenever economic power was nationalized the state had reservoirs of political power that could make socialism as oppressive as capitalism had been. State socialism, like corporate capitalism, had not guaranteed the equal distribution of power. This came to be Russell's central criticism of both corporate state capitalism and the Soviet Union.

For Russell, the good society was the one advocated by the anarchists; a society in which the production of goods and services was more or less mechanized, and in which the population consisted on the whole of free vagabonds. Such a society was not immediately feasible. Thus Russell proposed a compromise that was feasible and would take us in the direction of anarchism — guild socialism.

Guild socialism had existed in England since the first decade of this century as an alternative to Marxism and state socialism. According to its program, industrial society would be decentralized. Industry as a whole would be owned by the people, but each plant would be governed and managed by those who worked in it. Each plant would be autonomous, but they would all be associated with one another in some sort of confederation. Each unit in this society would be small enough to ensure that the individuals in it would be equal participants in the governing of their society. Russell was enthusiastic about these schemes for through them the sense of powerlessness that gripped the masses in modern society would be overcome:

> By a share in the control of smaller bodies, a man might regain some of that sense of personal opportunity and responsibility which belonged to the citizen of the city state in ancient Greece and mediaeval Italy.[60]

Russell believed he had broken with both traditional and modern liberalism through his advocacy of socialism and a decentralized society. The concept of a decentralized society, with a devolution of power, linked him to the political ideology of the New Left.

In one of the most curious sentences in his autobiographies, Russell claims that the First World War cured him of puritanism. At first glance this seems like a rather eccentric reaction to the carnage of 1914-1918. It did, however, follow from his notion of the repressed society, in which the discipline of modern industrial life had created a certain instinctual frustration that made men long for war and adventure. He was clearly influenced by James' notion of a moral equivalent for war, and shared with Freud (at least the Freud of *Civilization and its Discontents*) a vision of the human psyche as the battleground between the death wish and eros. The war had demonstrated that mankind would either find erotic happiness or destroy itself. It is against the background of these theories that Russell's popular books, *The Conquest of Happiness* and *Marriage and Morals*, should be read. They are political tracts for the liberation of eros in order that mankind would desire to live.

Russell attempted to make his most decisive break with

traditional and modern liberalism in his theories of psychology. He attacked it at its source, the theory of human nature. In C.B. MacPherson's phrase, liberalism held a theory of possessive individualism in which the individual competed in a free market in order to maximize his possessions. The basis of this theory was a concept of individuals activated by self-interest. Russell took the central concept of this liberalism to be desire, some desires being self-regarding and others being other-regarding. From this point of view, each individual pursued definite ends in accordance with his desires, and the problem of political philosophy was to define a system that would allow society to intervene and suppress the expression of desire against other individuals.

Russell's starting point was a theory of impulse. Unlike desires, impulses were pre-rational and were not directed towards any particular object. Impulses were either creative or possessive. Possessive impulses were directed towards material objects and put men in conflict with one another; while creative impulses were directed towards goods, the possession of which would not diminish other men's possessions. Impulses towards accumulating property put people in conflict with one another, whereas impulses towards creating poetry did not. Governing this structure is a central impulse that is the dominant principle of growth in each individual.

This theory of impulse was called Freudian by Russell and others, and through it Russell believed he had made the deeper layers of the individual psyche relevant to political theory. The whole set of concepts is difficult to deal with for Russell does not offer sufficient empirical evidence or even illustrations for his theory. What is striking, however, is the manner in which the traditional liberal concept of the relationship between the individual and society is altered. Through the theory of impulse, society is no longer regarded as an arena or marketplace for the maximization of possessions. Society becomes an environment for nourishing creative impulses. Indeed, the good society is to be judged according to its capacity to stimulate creativity. According to Wollheim, through this concept, Russell gave political theory a goal, an end, a measure whereby the good society could be judged.[61].

Russell attempted to reconstitute society from its very foundations. He had renounced classical liberalism's alliance with capitalism and the new liberalism's panacea of welfare through a powerful centralized state. This rejection was a corollary of Russell's refusal to adopt Marxism.

In the sixties, Russell's writings became associated with a post-Stalinist, even post-Marxist, socialism. In spite of his elaborate theorizing and the transition from liberalism to socialism, Russell was still primarily a liberal. This was so even though the closest approximation to the sort of society Russell had envisioned would surely be the socialist state of Czechoslovakia during the few brief weeks in 1968 under Dubcek before it was crushed by Soviet tanks.[62] The Czech society was socialist in the sense that all the means of production were in the hands of the people, but it was also free in the sense that it had a free press, freedom of speech, and so on. In addition to this, there were moves towards decentralizing industry, workers' control and other measures that Russell had advocated.

Once before, Russell had welcomed the new society that he hoped for; it was also a society that had been created by socialist revolution, Bolshevik Russia. Russell greeted Lenin's seizure of power with enormous enthusiasm, thinking that the Leninist slogan of "all power to the Soviets" could be taken at face value. "The world grows more full of hope every day" he wrote to Clifford Allen:

> The Bolsheviks delight me. I easily pardon their sacking of the Constituent Assembly if it at all resembles the House of Commons. Although in theory they are orthodox Marxists, in practice they are syndicalists.[63]

Russell's judgement that the Bolsheviks were not orthodox Marxists was mistaken, but it does show us the strength with which he yearned for libertarian socialism.

While Russell's version of socialism with a human face owed a great deal to a liberal fundamentalism, it retained a number of the problems and ambiguities of that philosophy. In the end, what Russell proposed was a society with a socialist body and a liberal soul.

The basis for this judgement is a formula that is repeated in almost every one of Russell's books dealing with human affairs. *Political Ideals* begins with the assertion that "political ideals must be based upon ideals for the individual life. . . . There is nothing for the politician to consider outside or above the various men and women and children who compose the world." In an earlier unpublished manuscript, "On the Democratic Ideal," he specifically rejected the concept of one ideal for the whole of society. This would "crush initiative and individuality." He opposed "one ideal for all men" and called for a "separate ideal for each separate man." A good deal of Russell's writing is devoted to upholding this formulation and to discrediting its opposite, the concept of a social whole somehow considered separately from its atomic parts. The scorn and abuse that he directed against Hegel is usually on this point. Hegel was accused of being the main protagonist for totalitarianism.[64]

The tenacity with which Russell defended his own individualist ideal separates him from most proponents of socialist theory. In one of his earliest essays, "On the Jewish Question," Karl Marx claims that the crucial distinction between liberal concepts of emancipation and socialist ones is that in the former individuals are emancipated while in the latter, society, and man the species, is liberated.

This point, though seemingly abstract and pedantic at first glance, disturbed even Russell's closest associates in guild socialism. The suspicion that for Russell guild socialism was a mask for liberalism was voiced by G.D.H. Cole, the leading theoretician of the guilds, who wrote Russell, "You do not give these [socialist] principles the same key position, and you still dwell mainly on a contract man vs the state, which seems to us obsolete."[65] This conflict on a point of abstract theory gave a completely different coloration to Russell's concept of guild socialism from that of Cole and the socialists. Russell wanted decentralization of society so that power could be shared. Cole emphasized the decentralization of the corporate economy, but still conceived of the guilds as having a relationship to the central authorities that made a coherent society possible. Russell agreed with this, but wanted the decentralization to include far more than economic units. He wanted guilds to exist for professions, religious bodies, service clubs and virtually everything that could be identified as a group. The emphasis for him was on the break-up of power:

> The diffusion of power both in the political and the economic sphere, instead of its concentration in the hands of officials and captains of industry, would generally diminish the opportunity for acquiring the habit of command out of which the desire for the exercise of tyranny is apt to spring.°°

In spite of broad agreement on the necessity for decentralization, Russell's concept begins to look more and more like a vast expansion of the liberal system of checks and balances. Society virtually disappears into an unfathomable network of guilds. He had devised what looks like a democratic fundamentalism and through it we come close to the old liberal concept of individuals rather than guilds competing to diminish one another's power. That is to say, bringing together Russell's proposals for guilds we cannot help but suspect that he saw them as a guerrilla tactic for keeping society out of the reach of its rulers.

The question of a socialist concept of freedom is a difficult one and not one that I propose to address in this essay except to point out the problems in one approach; that is, the assertion that socialism must be redefined on an individualist basis. In Russell's writings, the hostility to man or men in collectivities is so intense that it is unique in socialist thinking. An instance of this is his violent hatred of nationalism, a hatred that persists in his writing until the last five years of his life. Most socialists are prepared to make a distinction between reactionary and progressive nationalism. Russell did not. According to him, nationalism might in its first phase be a movement of the oppressed against tyranny, but so long as it remained nationalist it must ultimately become the oppression of someone else. Nationalism was for him an outmoded tribal instinct that postulated the enmity of all groups outside the primary one. He pointed to Poland of the twenties and thirties as an illustration of what he meant. The liberation of Poland had been the inspiration and one of the primary liberal causes of the nineteenth century. The liberated Poland in the 1930s was a dictatorship. Russell was brutally consistent on this point; even while writing as a socialist he warned that socialism within a nationalist framework is more dangerous than capitalist nationalism because socialism heals class antagonism and makes societies more cohesive for war. His daughter regarded Russell's anti-nationalism as the one fanatical element in his makeup. She says although he loved England, Russell was accustomed to repeat in scorn the famous verse: "Breathes there the soul with heart so dead, that never to himself has said, this is my own my native land."

Russell defined nationalism as:

a passion which has an instinctive root, namely rivalry between different groups. . . . Industrialism has rendered this instinct no longer useful and has at the same time immensely stimulated it.[67]

The difficulty here is that Russell defines every collective passion in the same way. Again, as a socialist, he stated in *Political Ideals:*

Men combine in groups to attain more strength in the scramble for material goods, and loyalty to the group spreads a halo of quasi-idealism round the central impulse of greed. Trade unions and the Labour party are no more exempt from this vice than other parties and other sections of society.[68]

When we consider Russell's vision of society as an aggregate of individuals rather than as a whole organism, separate from individuals, it seems at first that he is saying that collectivities have no independent existence. I am convinced, however, that if we were to examine all Russell's statements on collectivities a theory of socialization would emerge that held that they do indeed have an independent existence, they transform people so that once men combine into groups they turn into homicidal lunatics. This gives Russell a fundamental problem.[69] Society must be regenerated but who is going to do it? It must be some sort of collective human effort, but since collectivities are insane (and there is no other way of describing Russell's theory of collectivities), this collective effort must be viewed with suspicion. The original generation of liberals in the eighteenth century could get around this problem by claiming that they were not reconstituting society but merely removing some of the authoritarian obstacles to its proper functioning. Russell called for a complete effort of reconstruction. As is often the case, he is the best spokesman for his dilemma. In a letter to Constance Malleson, he agonized on this very problem:

> I know that for collective action the individual must be turned into a machine. But in these things, though my reason may force me to believe in them, I can find no inspiration. It is the individual soul that I love, in its loneliness, in its hopes and fears, its quiet impulses and sudden devotions. It is such a long journey from this to armies, states and officials. . . .[70]

The degree to which a fundamentalist individualism is embedded in Russell's social theory even affects the psychological basis upon which it rests. Possessive impulses are related to material things, they put men into conflict and are therefore bad. Now, what is the theoretical status of the political impulse, the desire to join a group or party to build a good society? Here Russell puts us in a quandary. The impulse to join is obviously suspect, but the desire to build a good society involves us with material things and brings us into conflict with others. Can such a collectivity ever be creative? Obviously not! Indeed, it seemed that Russell's theory of impulse, including as it did a central impulse of growth, implied a certain kind of society. One might expect an elaborate and even poetic description of institutions feeding this "central impulse." This was, after all, the great theme of Greek political theory. All that we learn from Russell, however, is that this growth is hindered by any kind of force, whether discipline, or authority, or fear of the tyranny of public opinion, or the necessity for engaging in some totally uncongenial occupation. Once again, it was G.D.H. Cole who was baffled by the theory of the completely depoliticized individual. He wrote Russell:

> I said you were not a political intellect, you seem to me to be a . . . philosopher King who asks of politics that they should not disturb you or anyone else who desires to live a non-political life.[71]

Another socialist who heard Russell expound his ideas and was baffled by them was the young student Mao Tsetung, who heard Russell lecture in China in 1920. He wrote to a friend that Russell's theories were naive:

> My argument pertains not merely to the impossibility of a society without power or organization. I should like to mention only the difficulties in the way of the establishment of such a form of society and its final attainment . . . my present viewpoint on absolute liberalism, anarchism and even democracy is that these things are fine in theory but not in practice.[72]

At the beginning of this chapter, I stated that in theory science and scientific organization were for Russell the means to attain the free society. But to state that science is a means requires some concrete explanation of how it is a means. For Russell it was self-evident that scientific organization created the collectivities he dreaded. It made men act like machines not individuals. This left him with the problem of how organized men could bring about the desired free society. What Russell advocated above all, and what liberalism in all its forms had failed to provide, was a combination of individual freedom and power or, as he called it, a new freedom of initiative. Failure to provide this freedom would turn industrial societies, socialist and capitalist, into prisons.

All Russell desired could only be accomplished by the "organized men" whom he distrusted. But since the free individual and the organized man were incompatible, we find that Russell was sinking into an insoluble problem.

III

SCIENCE AS ORGANIZATION

The free man and organized mass man are, in Russell's writings, antithetical to one another. Many thinkers who come to this conclusion retire into art or philosophy, for in modern times such a conclusion means that there is an insoluble antagonism between the free man and the world. Russell is, from time to time, on the brink of this conclusion and the fact that this possibility haunted him for most of his life is evident in "A Free Man's Worship" (1903). This is an essay in which Russell counsels free men not to build new societies but to build spiritual homes.

However, it was impossible for an activist such as Russell to remain permanently with such a conclusion. Russell did not feel that philosophically he could remove himself from the cave of human affairs for long, and the problem of the means of organizing society scientifically preoccupied him for almost the whole of his life. The problem was to show that this organization could be one in which freedom could flourish.

The writings in which organization or the scientifically organized society dominate his thought appeared during two periods. The first is from about 1889 to 1901 and includes his first published book. He then rebelled against the very concept of organized society, in ways that I have already shown, to become a spokesman for libertarian socialism until the early 1920s. Then, influenced by his visit to revolutionary Russia and China of the 1920s and disgusted by the impotence of the League of Nations, the problem of organization on a global scale dominated his writings until the late 1950s. Russell's preoccupation with world order became paramount as he wished to lay the foundations for a global society, but his ideas threatened his aspiration for freedom in a critical way.

Russell continued to struggle to maintain a concept of freedom in the light of the necessities that scientific technique imposed. He did so with difficulty, however, so that in the end the two great themes of the liberal tradition that he represented became problematic to one another. Russell managed to become both a prophet and a priest, a libertarian and a technocrat. He was a representative of tendencies that were at war with one another but that were sometimes held together by his willpower alone. The German poet Goethe once called Hamlet a beautiful soul in whom an oak had grown. Something similar could be said of Russell. In his heart he was an anarchist, but the great oak of science had taken root and all but strangled his libertarian principles. Russell's problem was that he had seen that the greater organization of mankind was inevitable and even necessary; and that such an organization meant deep incursions into individual freedom. At the same time he tried to show that some sort of organization of human affairs was the completion of the programme of liberalism. This effort threw him into a turmoil of contradictions.

Russell resisted the idea of science as merely an instrument of power. When he wrote about science he carefully distinguished between science as a disinterested theoretical activity whose sole object was knowledge, and scientific organization as praxis, as a way of ordering human society. He insisted on the epistemological validity of this distinction as well as its moral necessity. In his purely philosophical writings, therefore, he opposed operationalism, pragmatism and all those philosophies that regard science simply as a set of concepts through which we can manipulate nature. He was especially hostile to American pragmatism, and I believe that a thorough study of the relationship between Russell and John Dewey is long overdue. Pragmatism, according to Russell, had rejected the most important notion of science as disinterested theoretical truth. Science was the only means that mankind had discovered for gaining knowledge of the world outside of itself. The intensity with which Russell insisted upon this is often overlooked, as is the hostility with which he regarded pragmatism. His words, however, are clear.

Science as a way of ordering human affairs was becoming a misfortune because it had made nation states drunk with power. Certain philosophies had encouraged this. These were mainly philosophies that Russell referred to as power philosophies, such as that of Nietzsche, Fascism and American Pragmatism. His chapter on Dewey in his history of philosophy closes with the judgement that Dewey's was a "power philosophy" that opened the door to a "certain kind of madness — the intoxication with power which invaded philosophy with Fichte, and to which modern men whether philosophers or not are prone."[73] He continued, "I am persuaded that this intoxication is the greatest danger of our time, and that any philosophy which unintentionally contributes to it is increasing the danger of vast social disaster."[74]

Russell maintained the power of manipulation that science gives is not its essence. In an early essay, "The Place of Science in a Liberal Education," Russell disparages the view of science based on its "sensational triumphs," arguing that it is "the system of constructed knowledge which is the intrinsic value of the scientific habit of mind."[75] For Russell, the study of science gives a knowledge of reality that should produce a result quite different from the results of technology. Scientific theories are subject to being tested by reality. The practice of science is the most perfect manifestation of reason, which is "the endeavour to find out the truth of any matter with which we are concerned as opposed to the endeavour to prove to ourselves what we desire to be true." Science is the formation and testing of concepts according to a method that is indifferent to human desires, and it presents a reality that is indifferent to those desires. One canot help but contrast this austere sense of what science yields us as knowledge with the sense of what science can yield in benefits to mankind. Russell presents this broader benefit in his more libertarian prose. In that literature the world is open to innumerable alternatives, whereas in his writings on science an unmistakable note of stoic resignation dominates. Russell praised Spinoza for his stoic ethic and in the first volume of his autobiography spoke with great passion of Joseph Conrad, who, according to Russell, had written with conviction of the limitations of man and all his hopes.

It is true that in the course of time Russell wrote of science as a method of enquiry in less metaphysical tones. The sense of the smallness of man before the infinity of the universe that one finds in his essay, "A Free Man's Worship," becomes less acute in later works. But Russell always insists that, unlike the power philosophies of the twentieth century and the various subjectivist philosophies, scientific enquiry is about objective fact. Subjective fantasies and desires are always limited by science. This is, for Russell, the important feature of the correspondence theory of truth; that truth must correspond with fact. "If I say of something that it is so when in fact it is, nothing subjective enters such a judgement."[76] Moreover, as that knowledge is so tied to fact, it inspires humility since "a respect for objective truth is apt to operate as a brake on the illusions of unlimited power that spring from the subjectivist bias." By writing in this fashion Russell, whether intentionally or not, is presenting more than a technical epistemological theory. He speaks of reason in a sort of classical sense of the knowledge wherein man knows his limits. Whether or not "knowledge of fact" can bear such burdens is not my concern here. My aim is to indicate that for Russell science as truth somehow acts as an alternative to the pervasive notion of science as power.

It would not be far-fetched to say that, for Russell, scientific knowledge is the capacity to yield to necessity and, in this sense, reason plays the traditional role of that which stands in opposition to desire. Something of this sense of yielding to necessity is an essential ingreident in Russell's view of science as a practical activity. We might say: scientific technique means organization; organization adversely affects freedom; but organization is necessary and inevitable. Thus, we shall begin to trace the manner in which Russell became a prophet of the expansion of technology and organization and how it affected him as a prophet of freedom.

Coexisting with these cautions about science and power is a strong streak of Bonapartism. In an important way, Russell simply continued in the tradition of the philosophy of the Enlightenment. Philosophers, it will be recalled, looked to absolutist monarchs as agents of the society that they desired to bring into being. Russell often slipped into that tradition which held that liberty could be established by force. His grandfather was a supporter of Napoleon and Russell himself once remarked that Europe would be a happier place had Napoleon been victorious. It is not recognized how deeply this Bonapartism was felt by Russell, or how persistently it coexisted with writings inspired by anarchism.

Russell maintained that the advance of scientific technique is both desirable and necessary. In *The Scientific Outlook*, he reminds his readers that "We are accustomed, in our own day, to protests against the empire of machinery and eloquent yearnings for a return to simpler days."[77] He says the yearnings for the return to nature are as old as the Chinese philosopher Lao-tzu. In our own day, such a return would mean the death by starvation of ninety percent of the population. In every age, Russell argued, the return to nature has a different meaning. Lao-tzu poured scorn on "the taming of horses, and the arts of the potter and carpenter." A later supporter of the return to nature, Rousseau, advocated returning to those very conditions that Lao-tzu had denounced. "To Rousseau, the carpenter would have seemed the very epitome of honest toil. 'Return to nature' means, in practice, return to those conditions to which the writer in question was accustomed in his youth."[78]

In practice, however, Russell was not always enthusiastic about those advances he accepted as inevitable. A good deal of his writing consists of exhortations to yield to necessary evils as, for example, when he exhorted a New York audience: "I retain the tastes and prejudices of an old fashioned liberal. I like democracy, I like individual liberty, but it is dangerous to allow one's prejudices to dictate one's opinions."[79]

Russell's wrestling with the problem of organization, its necessity and its impact on liberty, is part of the earliest examples we have of his political thinking. In a document in the Bertrand Russell Archives at McMaster, "The Green Note Book," he presents a series of essays, perhaps for a tutor who was preparing him for a university entrance examination. They are largely on the subjects of liberalism, protest and socialism. These essays, written in 1889 when Russell was seventeen years old, reflect the ideological turmoil of the 1880s and 1890s, and in them Russell is already grappling with his lifelong theme of freedom or organization.

He began one of his essays by noting the instability of political science over the past century when "many ancient principles which have not been doubted from the time of the ancient Greeks have been overthrown."[80] He called for a flexible attitude towards the subject of government in view of the various competing theories, "most having a certain element of truth which causes their acceptance among a certain class of people."[81] In the subsequent discussions it is clear that the competing theories with which he was concerned were *laissez-faire* liberalism, as preached by Herbert Spencer, and socialism. In the essays he wavered between the two.

Russell recognized even then that liberalism in its original form could not be regarded as holy writ. Classical liberalism, as taught by Adam Smith, held that "Nature, if left to itself, will tend to prosperity and comfort."[82] This oversimplification had to be modified at a very early stage, according to Russell. In the light of Malthus's discovery, nature left to itself creates disastrous expansions of population. But, he continued, even if its original optimism were unwarranted, the principle of *laissez-faire* had, until then, been regarded on practical grounds as sound doctrine, and experience had taught that it was preferable to any alternatives. Russell's chief concern was that a new challenge had come from those who believed that men's lives could be improved by social legislation and government interference. "The rigid *laissez-faire* doctrine is now abandoned by all who have any connection with practical work."[83] He noted further that the state now recognized "hardly anything with which it may not interfere. It compels education, it regulates hours of labour, it forces landowners to sell their land to railways and even breaks leases."[84]

In one essay, Russell regarded this greater control as regrettable, but in another he acknowledged its necessity. In the first essay, he raised the familiar liberal complaint that state interference saps initiative and self-reliance. He admitted that there may be a great deal of pressure to accept socialism and there may be some benefits from it, but:

It is more likely ... to produce apathy and laziness among labourers; to make their work less efficient, to remove the stimulus to improve its foundation. It should then, be fought by all who wish sturdiness and energy to be maintained.[85]

In the second essay he felt obliged to reject the *laissez-faire* philosophy of Herbert Spencer on the grounds that it can be "more cruel in its operations than the most bloodthirsty of tyrants" and that "if a system would allow the continuance of such a state of things as existed formerly amongst factory hands, we are inclined to question the system."[86] So, although socialism might in certain respects be undesirable, "in some form or other [it] seems inevitably coming on, and although it is a retrograde movement it *may be a necessary stage in the progress towards perfect liberty when as among Swift's Houyhnhnms, government shall no longer be necessary, but all shall work together for the good of the whole.*"[87] This last formula is remarkable because it expresses, and can be used as the motto for, Russell's political thought as it matured.

That the challenge of socialism remained important is

demonstrated by the fact that Russell joined the Fabians in 1897. In the year 1895, while he was still undecided between devoting his life to politics or to philosophy, he spent a year in Germany to observe and study the German Social Democratic party. The result of this year of research was his first published book, *German Social Democracy*. In it he discussed not only the party but the political ideas that guided it — the theories of Karl Marx. The book is interesting in several respects. First, it is a useful study of the German Socialist party; second, it is Rusell's first major statement on Marxism. (Many of his leading contentions were not changed in any of his later writings on this subject.) Finally, it shows that even at this early stage, the synthesis between the liberal notion of freedom and the socialist demand for organization had become very problematic for him.

Though his attitude to Marxism was skeptical, he was more sympathetic to it than is commonly supposed.[88] He believed that the *Communist Manifesto* was the greatest political pamphlet that had ever been written. Russell praised Marx for having presented industrial society as it was viewed by the wage earner. He believed one of Marx's central theses, the Law of the Concentration of Capital, was a genuine contribution to knowledge, a contribution that carried Marxism beyond classical economics. As a man of science, Russell felt bound to accept the concequences of organization. He rejected all Marx's ideas associated with the inevitability of class struggle but accepted the inevitability of greater organization.

Russell's method of analysis was carefully to separate what he regarded as scientifically established by Marx, from what he regarded as Marx's misconceptions. The unscientific elements, in Russell's view, were inspired by Marx's political interest in fomenting revolutionary class struggle. Russell saw the theory of the inevitability of revolution as a quasi-scientific religious creed that should be dispensed with. He argued that at the centre of this creed were two biases, one indeed revolutionary, but the other fatalistic. The former, derived from the Hegelian mataphysic rather than from science, was based on the conviction that fundamental historical changes must be revolutionary rather than evolutionary. This is so because, in Marxism, change is dialectical and dialectic is derived from logic rather than observation. "Logical ideas are clear and sharply defined against one another and incapable of Darwinian evolution."[89] The other element, fatalism, is described by Russell as something of a counter to the first, for it provided the possibility of day-to-day endurance when all odds pointed against the achievement of the program: "There is almost an oriental tinge in the belief shared by all orthodox Marxists that capitalist society is doomed and the advent of a communist society a foreordained necessity."[90]

In spite of these criticisms, it is most important to note that Russell was still prepared to claim that Marx had made serious advances in the study of economics. The most relevant discovery in Marxism, for Russell, was the Law of the Concentration of Capital. According to this law, an economy with a large number of small competing firms would gradually evolve into one characterized by huge monopolies. This prediction seemed to be coming true in the Europe of the 1890s with the rise of cartels and corporations. Marx was right in pointing out that the competitive struggles essential to classical economics would not continue forever, for some competitors would win. Russell saw this law as describing what was actually taking place before everyone's eyes in the late nineteenth century. The development was, in his view, inevitable and beneficial, for only through such concentrations of industry could there be a world of abundance.

In accepting this law, Russell did not adopt Marx's scenario as it stood. He did not believe that the destruction of capitalism would come in the way Marx prophesied. On the contrary, he believed that the rise of the joint stock companies (corporations) would mean the expansion of the middle class. This class would include a new technical intelligentsia crucial to the new forms of production. This class would include new levels of management who would run different sections of the corporations, for in a sense each coporation would consist of a large number of small firms.

Finally, even the workers could become part of the middle class, for their trade unions and other associations would, through their investments, develop an interest in the well-being of the capitalist system. Socialism, if it came, would be gradual. Circumstances might from time to time dictate that government take over certain industries until a time arrived when it found itself in control of the economy. This was hardly the apocalypse predicted in *Das Kapital*. The process would be "a gradual organic development instead of the discontinuous dialectical change which Social Democracy expects."[91]

In the preface to the 1965 edition of *German Social Democracy*, Russell claimed that he wrote it as an orthodox liberal. It seems more the work of an orthodox Fabian, for it accepts the inevitability of something akin to socialism but not the inevitability of the class struggle. The Fabians believed that socialism would come through the enlightened administration of a bureaucratic elite, even if this elite did not consist of socialists. Russell was saying the same thing with a thoroughly aristocratic viewpoint permeating the entire work. Russell, as a member of the liberal ruling class of England, was really observing the consequences of the regime of the unenlightened rulers of Germany.

The doctrine of class war, which he rejected on economic grounds, made sense to him in the German environment. The German workers were, in fact, oppressed by brutal Prussian officialdom. This is why he thought the revolutionary element in Marxism appealed to them. It also explained why the Social Democratic Party adopted what he regarded as an extreme and unwise form of democracy in their program. He pointed out that they called for the election of even minor administrative officials. Russell was not, at this stage, a libertarian socialist, and he could not sympathize with such a demand as it did not take sufficient account of the need for expertise. But for Russell, such an irrational demand was understandable in the light of the oppressiveness of German officialdom. In its closing pages, the central purpose of *German Social Democracy* becomes clear. It is an appeal to the ruling class. "I would wish in conclusion to emphasize the immense importance, for the internal peace of the nation, of every spark of generosity and emancipation from class consciousness in the governing and propertied classes. This more than anything else is to me the lesson of German politics."[92] In true Fabian fashion, he held that the Bonapartes would be the upper classes of England.

In the broadest sense, Russell was confronting, for the first time, what he was to call the "problem of organization." In this book he made no attempt to reconcile this problem with the freedom of the individual. In fact, he deliberately avoided the issue. Near the end of the book he asked, "Are the demands contained in this inner core of socialism in themselves possible or desirable?" In answer to his own question he was evasive: "This involves the whole controversy as to socialism or individualism, and . . . I have no wish to enter on a controversial question for whose discussion I have not the necessary knowledge."[93]

A few years after writing this book he underwent the dramatic change that I have documented earlier. Russell lost interest in the Fabians and every form of social engineering and, until a few years after the end of World War I, wrote primarily about the quality of society and its ability to enhance individual freedom. His immediate reaction to Fabianism and every other form of social utilitarianism was characteristically violent. Though he remained on friendly terms with the Fabian leaders, the Webbs, his judgement on them was harsh. After one of their visits he wrote Murray:

> We had a visit from the Webbs in Normandy and I minded them more than usual. They have a competent way of sizing up a cathedral and pronouncing on it with an air of authority and an evident feeling that the L.C.C. [London County Council] would have done it better. They take all the colour out of life and make everything one cares for turn into dust and ashes.[94]

In the aftermath of World War I, however, the theme of organization of human affairs began to re-emerge and to take on a new importance. During the First World War, while

Russell was developing his quasi-anarchistic social philosophy, there was a hint of what was to come from an appeal to the American President, Woodrow Wilson, calling for an imposed peace. "The United States government has the power not only to compel the European governments to make peace but also to reassure the populations by making itself the guarantor of peace."[95] Russell obviously did not consider whether the United States government would also become the guarantor of libertarian socialism. Or perhaps he had, because the moment that the Americans began sending their troops to England, he wrote an article saying that they would act as strike-breakers. For this he was subsequently imprisoned.

As the years wore on, Russell began to construct an epic scenario that included the organization of human affairs by some overwhelming power. The epic, as it appears in a number of books and articles, has a Hegelian ring to it. In the epic mankind would be coerced into some order both political and economic, that would allow a free society to emerge on a global scale. Russell gave up his anarchism, but a good deal of the rest of his libertarianism remained intact, including guild socialism. The world historical power that would accomplish this, he eventually concluded, was the United States of America. What he suggested was that there was a long dialectical epic that might last for centuries in which the world would first be ordered and then later devolve into a global order of guild socialism. The employment of force and coercion would, even if it lasted for centuries, only be temporary, a mere stepping stone to freedom. Here we have the return of the thought that had first appeared in the notebooks of the young student, that mankind would go through a period of force in order to achieve the freedom of Swift's Houyhnhnms.

The first context in which this idea began to mature was with reference to the Bolsheviks. Russell, even after learning that Lenin and Trotsky were indeed not syndicalists and were imposing the dictatorship of the proletariat on the Russian people, still supported them vigorously. In a speech to guildsmen union members in 1920, he declared that:

The dictatorship of the proletariat is professedly a transitional condition, a wartime measure, justified while the remnants of the old bourgeois class are struggling to promote counter revolution . . . I think that there is something a bit pedantic in applying to the circumstances of Russia the sort of principles that are valid for ourselves in ordinary periods. Russia could only be saved by a strong will, and it is doubtful whether a strong will could have saved it without dictatorship in some form.[96]

A short time later, Russell went with a delegation of labour leaders to see revolutionary Russia first hand. Russell wrote his observations in a series of articles which were turned into a book, *Bolshevism: Practice and Theory of.* This book was one of the turning points in Russell's development, the evidence of his disillusionment with the Soviet experiment. The book became one of the sacred texts of the Cold War and during that period Russell was hailed as one of the few intellectuals of the left who had not been hoodwinked by the Soviets. Russell's one-time colleague, David Horowitz, however, reads it as basically a pro-Soviet text, and there is some justification for this view. One piece of evidence for this position is the introduction to a later book, written after Russell's so-called disillusionment, in which he says, "I agree with the Bolsheviks more than with the American magnates."[97]

Horowitz overstates the case. Russell's tone in the articles is one of frankness and balance, but his argument should be read carefully, for Russell does not disagree with the necessity for a temporary dictatorship of the proletariat.

Russell believed in something more complex and subtle; that a dictatorship of the proletariat, organized under Marxist concept of class struggle, was likely to be permanent. Socialism needs some liberal hope if the dictatorship is gradually to crumble. Later, in reviewing Bukharin's *The A.B.C. of Communism*, he ridiculed the doctrine of a temporary dictatorship under Marxist auspices:

The dictatorship is to last a long time, but at last when the bourgeoisie has died out the bureaucrats, who will have acquired a centralized state control such as has never been known before, are to abdicate voluntarily.[98]

This, however, did not mean that the dictatorship of the proletariat was illegitimate under any circumstances; rather, one should be careful about what theory one uses in order to justify it. Russell for his part continued to believe that this dictatorship was necessary under the conditions in early Bolshevik Russia. In the opening pages of his account, he declared that "I believe that socialism is necessary to the world, and I believe that the heroism of Russia has fired men's hopes in a way which was essential . . . Bolshevism deserves the gratitude and admiration of the progressive part of mankind."[99] He vigorously defended the Leninists on the grounds that they had to cope with civil war and they were surrounded and threatened with drowning in a sea of capitalism. Russell also pointed out that Russia was exceptionally dependent on foreign capital and that the hostility of foreign powers meant that a will of iron had to rule Russia. "Russia is a backward country, not yet ready for the methods of equal cooperation.... In Russia the methods of the Bolsheviks are probably more or less unavoidable, at any rate I am not prepared to criticize them in their broad lines."[100]

Russell encountered in Soviet Russia and then later in China the phenomenon of societies that had to undergo vast structural changes in order to industrialize. This phenomenon was to become necessary on a global scale. "Bolshevism may go under in Russia, but even if it does it will spring up again elsewhere, since it is ideally suited to an industrial population in distress."[101]

In *The Prospects of Industrial Civilization*, he expands this view and develops it more fully. The transition from pre-industrial to industrial society, according to Russell, must always be accomplished by force. This was equally true of early capitalism and present-day communism. The reason for this was that the process of early capital accumulation, the building of systems of transportation and energy, always meant that present satisfactions must be postponed for future ones. "Russian industry, under the Bolsheviks," he wrote, "reminds one of English industry a hundred years ago."[102] The Soviet commissars were fulfilling the same function as the English capitalists of the early nineteenth century. That both were necessary was obvious to Russell for he argued that, had the English working class been consulted about bringing industry to England in the eighteenth century, they would most likely have opposed it. In the interests of bringing industry to pre-industrial societies, freedom has to be postponed, but, it might also be argued, that freedom could be reinstated as a society reaches a certain level of economic development. The problem of economic development was not the only one that Russell believed should be solved by coercion; there was also the problem of world government. Even at this stage we can detect something of a disturbance in the way in which Russell views these matters. The underlying thought appears to be that coercion is necessary when dealing with human collectivities. The theory I alluded to in the last chapter applies here in the case of economic development. Individuals are rational but collectivities are not; therefore, they must be dealt with through coercion.

I have already mentioned that Russell regarded nationalism as the great evil of our time. Nationalism is what chiefly succeeded in transforming individuals into collectivities and men into lunatics. Russell was always quite graphic and vivid on this point. "Devotion to the nation is perhaps the most widespread religion of the present age. Like the ancient religions it demands its persecutions, its holocausts, its lurid heroic cruelties; like them it is noble, primitive, brutal and mad."[103] Nationalism has transformed science into a monster and inculcated large sections of humanity with a will to power. Reason, which increasingly means force, is needed to curb this madness. Russell's own words were:

> Shakespeare puts the "lunatic," the lover and the poet together as being of imagination all compact. The problem is to keep the lover and the poet without the

lunatic.[104]

As the twentieth century wore on, the lunatic and the nationalist became synonomous. The lunatic became modern man *per se*. The amount of force and organization necessary to control modern man grew to such an extent that it seems impossible to imagine the world order Russell devised could ever be transformed into a global democratic state.

By the late 1920s, after being disillusioned with the impotence of the League of Nations, Russell hoped that the Americans would play the world historical role of unifying the globe. He applauded the expansion of American capitalism and the various economic programs that brought Europe and other parts of the world into the hands of American capital. At this time Russell informed socialists that international finance was the main hope for mankind. Russell always worried lest the Americans botch up the job and provoke worldwide rebellion against capitalism. He would have preferred that America become a socialist country. Whatever the case, one thing seemed certain: "Owing to man's folly world government will only be established by force."[105]

Russell still regarded this programme as necessary to realize his liberal ideals and he hoped that it would culminate in guild socialism. The numerous strains that this belief imposed are evident in an unpublished manuscript he wrote in 1943 entitled, "An Outline of Political Philosophy." This work sets out to "deduce from an ethic essentially identical with transitional liberalism practical conclusions as regards economics, international relations, war, and the limits of governmental power, which shall have the same relevance to our world as Locke's political philosophy had to the world of his day."[106] As we read on, we discover that the deductions include the dismantling of capitalism and industry, the growth of guild socialism and, finally, the establishment of an international authority. Russell did not expect that this would be the result of the Second World War. He believed another war was necessary, so, in the middle of World War II, Russell was already preparing for World War III.

In a number of visionary writings Russell began to imagine how the society he hoped for would arise from the conquest of the globe by any one nation. Sometimes he predicted that this take-over would begin to happen in the middle of the twenty-first century:

> Assuming a monopoly of armed forces established by the victory of one side in a war between the U.S. and the U.S.S.R., what sort of world will result? In either case, it will be a world in which successful rebellion will be impossible, although, of course, sporadic assassinations will still be liable to occur. The concentration of all important weapons in the hands of the victors will make them irresistible, and there will therefore be a secure peace. Even if the dominant nation is completely devoid of altruism, its leading inhabitants at least will achieve a very high degree of material comfort, and will be freed from the tyranny of fear. They are likely, therefore, to become gradually more good natured, and less inclined to persecute. Like the Romans, they will in the course of time extend citizenship to the vanquished. There will then be a true world state and it will be possible to forget that it owed its origins to conquest.[107]

This is a peculiar, if not desperate, dialectic for a man who had already argued against Marxism that the dictatorship of the proletariat would never come to an end because those who had the habit of power would never give it up voluntarily.

Even more peculiar is the argument used to support these speculations. Drawing examples from early modern history, he contended that democracy had not been possible until the contending powers of feudalism were overwhelmed by the mediaeval kings. The absolutist monarchs had to achieve political unity before democracy could evolve. The part of this argument that Russell left out was that democracy did not evolve; but was attained by force, through the English Civil War, the French Revolution and the democratic revolutions of the eighteenth century. The question remains, how is a new form of liberty to be achieved in the twenty-first century with a government "against whom no rebellion was possible"?

The issue of science also came to the fore in Russell's vision of the future. Russell had to face the problem of how he could support his abstract proposition that science was a means to the end he sought; that is, the means to attain the good society. From the perspective of history, this statement is hardly a self-evident one. There remains the traditional image of science as a tool and man as the operator or user of this tool. But it is certainly true that the tool becomes more than a means when it also changes the operator. This is especially evident if the operator is seen as something specific, for example, feudal society. Science and technology cannot be a tool for feudal society to achieve its ends. New systems of communication and transportation, and the growth of new classes that know how to use them, mean that, in the case of feudalism, scientific technique undermines and destroys the subject that incorporates it. According to Marx and Engels, the same is true of capitalism, for the driving force in Marxist theory is a demonstration that the development of scientific technology doomed capitalism. We already have examples that make this point. The question is, what kind of society provides the context in which science can become the tool? Ellul claims that there is no such social order and that technique undermines all it touches. For Russell, the only society in which science could become a means for the good society is a global one, a world state. He believed international coporations had rendered the nation state redundant. Under the auspices of the multinationals, science had become not a tool but a menace. Instead of providing leisure, the surplus time science makes available had been used in the production of weapons of destruction. Scientific technique can only once again become a possibility for good only after the nation state is abolished in favour of one unified world government.

In a tribute that Russell wrote for the philosopher Paul A. Schilpp,[108] he pointed out that to win mankind over to his own point of view it was important to show not only what evils can be avoided but what good men can hope for in a proper world.

We have already noted that the kind of good society Russell advocated was unlikely to grow out of the means he had envisaged as bringing it into being. It remains to see whether the conception of world government Russell advocated was consistent with his liberal hopes, and finally, whether there were some other conditions in the very organization of science that rendered these hopes impotent.

The world order that Russell sketched consisted of a government that had a monopoly of force, and a diversity of nation states that regulated their own affairs in all matters excepting war and peace. Russell sincerely hoped that local autonomy and cultural diversity would continue. The world government was to consist primarily of an executive branch, a military and a judiciary. This government's primary role was to be the enforcement of international agreements. The model of such a world order is found in neither Marx nor Locke, but in a philosopher of whom Russell was very critical, Hobbes. A government that crushes rebellions and enforces contracts is derived directly from the *Leviathan*. (Hobbes, however, in advocating such a regime did not advocate libertarian guild socialism.) Russell believed that world government should be federal but should have enormous powers, such as responsibility for global economic development. These powers are so the various national cultures of the world would have their power limited. The question arises, what in fact would all the national units of the world do? Would they have any substantial powers?

Among the various powers of world government, Russell inserted the power to object to nationalist propaganda and nationalist educational systems. What precisely he meant by "object" would certainly cause anyone entering such an arrangement a good deal of disquiet. When a government with overwhelming force and virtually unlimited power objects, its response could be unlimited.

Thus the world government would control military power, the global economy and national opinions. Such concepts, coming from a lover of freedom who flirted with anarchism, are so dismaying that one wonders whether

Russell's hatred for nationalism had driven him berserk.

This fear is confirmed if we examine Russell's discussion of Hobbes in his *History of Western Philosophy*. Russell objects quite strenuously to Hobbes's concept of a Leviathan, but he adds: "Every argument that he addresses in favour of government, insofar as it is valid at all, is valid in favour of international government." We must couple this statement with Russell's criticism of Hobbes's concept of government. He states first, "The reason that Hobbes gives for supporting the state, namely that it is the only alternative to anarchy, is, in the main, a valid one," but "the tendency of every government toward tyranny cannot be kept in check unless governments have some fear of rebellion."[109] Since the ability to crush any rebellion is the chief attribute of the world government, this sentence demonstrates that Russell could not synthesize his liberal hopes and his schemes for world order.

In a certain sense Russell seems to have feared that the nature of scientific organization and technique was making any philosophy of freedom invalid. In *The Scientific Outlook*, written in the early 1930s, he discusses directly the question of how the development of the industrial system has affected John Stuart Mill's concept of liberty. The principle which Mill had adopted, that the state had the right to interfere only in those actions where individuals harmed one another, has, according to Russell, become obsolete for "as society becomes more organic, the effects of men upon each other become more and more numerous and important."[110] Therefore there remains hardly anything that Mill's defence of liberty is applicable to. Russell says on "the one hand, modern technique makes society more organic; on the other hand modern sociology makes men more aware of the causal laws in virtue of which men's acts are useful or harmful to another man." "If liberty is justifiable at all," he goes on to argue, "we shall have to do it on the ground that the form of liberty is for the good of society as a whole, but not in most cases on the ground that the acts concerned affect nobody but the agent."[112] It is hard to imagine a more powerful argument against John Stuart Mill; indeed it might be called the most crucial argument against him.

In the rest of *The Scientific Outlook*, Russell shows that the affairs of mankind must inevitably fall into the hands of mandarin experts, whose power and authority are unmatched. A new hierarchy must inevitably sweep aside the dreams of liberty and equality that grew up in the nineteenth century. The only hope that Russell offers at the end of the book is that the new race of mandarins will have a humane education and will deal with human affairs with wisdom. Nowhere does he suggest how they can be checked by any social form.

Of course he continues as a staunch defender of freedom, but in his later writings Russell's argument does, in fact, shift from the defence of liberty as an intrinsic good, to a defence on utilitarian grounds. One of the arguments that he advances on a number of occasions is that free societies do not lose wars. Throughout Russell continued to write in favour of decentralization and the construction of a society that offered a great deal of scope for individual initiative and activity. But one can never escape the feeling that masses of men could not have the power to influence anything of great importance.

Authority and the Individual (1949) is an eloquent book in favour of a world in which power is shared among the population. It is a call for redistribution of power. But in this, as well as other books, one constantly finds expressions that indicate that this redistribution is limited to a feeling of power. For example, Russell advised his readers: "If our political thoughts are all concerned with vast problems and dangers of world catastrophe, it is easy to become despairing. But in relation to smaller problems — those of your own town, or your trade union, or the local branch of your political party for example — you can hope to have a successful influence."[113] Such expressions are quite common in Russell, indicating that there is an unresolved problem between a polity of power and a psychology of power.

One cannot pretend that the problems Russell was grappling with are easy ones or are problems that lend themselves to easy solutions. The problem of preserving human space in the context of modern technology is the problem of our era, and science is our peculiar destiny. Russell's hope for a society that is decentralized and consists of units resembling the ancient classical city states is a noble one. The difficulty is not that he has failed to find the means for bringing it into being, it is much greater. In contending, for example, with centralization versus decentralization, Russell becomes involved in something resembling schizophrenia. When his attention is focussed on the individual — his happiness, well-being and spontaneity — he insists on a society that is dismantled and will give this individual scope for initiative and a full life. When Russell turns his attention to the broader level of social existence — the great collectivities, nationalism, the threat of thermonuclear war — he insists on organization and all the draconian measures needed to bring it about. If one reads Russell carefully, the chief problem is that these two levels never seem to meet in a real engagement with one another. The two books I have just mentioned, *The Scientific Outlook* and *Authority and the Individual*, are good examples of this. The first shows the inevitable centralizing power of science, which is supported by very good arguments. The second is an eloquent plea for decentralization, but though it answers some of the general considerations of the first, it does not deal with the contentions of scientific outlook.

For instance, in *The Scientific Outlook* Russell demonstrates that the very complexity of scientific structures means that they will be managed by a priesthood of experts who have knowledge that is incommunicable to the masses. As an example he speaks of bankers dealing with complex matters of credit. In *Authority and the Individual*, he advocates that greater masses of people should be allowed to participate in human affairs, but he does not show how this participation will influence important global events.

Russell's Bonapartism arose from the fact that, as a relic of the aristocratic liberalism of an earlier age, he was appalled by the mass collectivities of modern civilization. He wanted such groupings dismantled but he did not want to set the clock back. He therefore hoped that some power would complete the homogenizing work and then go away. In this sense his work does not bring mankind closer to any solution of its problems; it merely confuses the problems.

Russell is important in that no matter how maverick he may seem, he illustrates a particular type of problem in the history of liberalism. Liberalism has governed by an ideal of freedom and by technocracies which manage society. These frequently come into conflict in spite of the fact that they are both manifestations of the same social philosophy. This conflict between science and freedom seems permanent. Within the same liberal civilization, schemes for ordering society more perfectly coexist with cultural revolts against that order. Hegel once said that the finite and the infinite seek each other and flee each other. The same can be said of liberalism when science and liberty seek each other and flee from each other.

EPILOGUE

It is a testimony to Russell's great vitality that the most controversial period of his life is the last one, from the late fifties until 1970. He was the subject of heated debate at the age of ninety-seven. During these years Russell was arrested for civil disobedience, acted as a self-appointed ombudsman for mankind, and established a war crimes tribunal to dramatize his opposition to the war in Vietnam. Much of Russell's activity is quite intelligible within the framework of the political philosophy that I have outlined in these pages, but some of it is not. I feel compelled to limit myself to raising problems without completely answering them until further information becomes available.

Many of Russell's admirers have found the last period of his life baffling for the wrong reasons. Many who imbibed their anti-communism and empiricism from Russell's writings of the late forties were astounded to see him associated with left-wing revolutionaries. His apparent transformation from an extreme hawk to an extreme dove confused some people and embittered others. C.L. Sulzberger, quoting in the *New York Times* the accusations of an author of a book on the war in Vietnam, wrote:

"No individual within the communist bloc or without was of more value to the N.L.F. [political expression of the

Viet Cong] in its externalization efforts than Bertrand Russell, the British philosopher. That he should have become such an unthinking transmission belt for the most transparent Communist lies . . . that he should have thrown over all objectivity, and accepted on an unsubstantiated basis virtually all statistics and statements supplied by the N.L.F. . . . is one of the great intellectual tragedies of our time."[114]

This is certainly an exaggeration, but it illustrates the passions that Russell's last crusades evoked.

The evolution of Russell's position in the late fifties is, in fact, a coherent one, and only in his last five years did he make any dramatic breaks with the principles that he had advocated for most of his life. That there were changes and inconsistencies in his political philosophy is true. But these occurred near the end and are to be found in his new acceptance of nationalism.

In the early years of the Cold War Russell's proposal to threaten the Soviet Union derived from his arguments for the need to establish a world government by force. He did not regard these proposals as part of an anti-communist crusade.

During all of the Cold War years, Russell feared anti-communism as a political creed. While he was a member of the Congress for Cultural Freedom, he became suspicious of its involvement in the Cold War and as early as May, 1953, he sent a letter to one of its officials maintaining that "it would be a mistake for me to be a sponsor of the American Committee for Cultural Freedom since at this distance I cannot know adequately what its actions are or whether they are such that I should wish to support."[115] His doubts about the American committee were occasioned by the fact that some of its members had attacked him for a letter he had published in the *Manchester Guardian*. In this letter he claimed that the Rosenbergs, who had been executed in America as spies for the Soviet Union, had been unjustly accused and were victims of political persecution. Russell's public and private writings remained hostile to Stalin's regime, but he was not a believer in the infallibility of the free world. A few years later, in April, 1956, still smarting from the *Guardian* episode, he wrote Stephen Spender: "The American Branch [of the Congress for Cultural Freedom] is in favour of cultural freedom for Russia and China but disapproves of it elsewhere."[116] This demonstartes that, in his own mind at least, Russell's hard line during the Cold War was not primarily ideological.

Russell's evolution from hawk to dove was not a dramatic, ideological one, but rather a logical response to new circumstances based on his previous convictions. Russell's hawkishness was inspired by his desire for world government. In the late forties he had felt that only the power of America could bring this about. By the early fifties both the United States and the Soviet Union had atomic weapons and therefore world government could only be brought about by negotiation between these super powers. Russell responded with his activities for peace and nuclear disarmament. But in his statements in the 1950s he still believed in the "balance of terror" between America and the U.S.S.R. and only advocated disarmament for the smaller powers. Specifically, he concentrated his energies on persuading the British people to dismantle their own nuclear establishment. Russell did not, at this time, nor did he in the future, ever advocate unilateral disarmament by either of the super powers. His goal was to stimulate negotiations between nuclear powers that would lead to a general disarmament. Russell brought together scientists from both sides of the Iron Curtain to make statements warning of the dangers of nuclear war. These meetings of scientists became known as the Pugwash Conferences.

Russell's activities for disarmament as well as his increasing tolerance of Marxists indicated to his critics that he had in fact altered his fundamental beliefs. Yet I know of no instance where he repudiated the criticisms of Marxism in the books that he had written earlier.[117] It should be remembered that in these books Russell emphasized that in underdeveloped countries Marxism has a certain legitimacy that it does not have in advanced countries. On the other hand, he was never unreservedly pro-American and it might be recalled that many of Russell's criticisms of the pragmatic philosophy of Dewey, which governed American liberalism, were far more severe than those that he levelled against Marxism.

The decisive change in Russell's post war attitude to America seems to have come when he concluded that Khrushchev was open to negotiation, but that the American government was dominated by a rabid and fanatical anti-communism. In 1958 Russell addressed open letters to Khrushchev and Eisenhower urging a spirit of compromise between the super powers. Khrushchev replied on behalf of the Russians and John Foster Dulles on behalf of the Americans. Russell's reaction was that "the righteously adamantine surface of Mr. Dulles' mind as shown in his letters filled me with greater foreboding that did the fulminations and sometimes contradictions of Mr. Khrushchev. The latter seemed to show some underlying understanding of alternatives and realities; the former none."[118]

Until this point, the changes in Russell's political sympathies were consistent with his fundamental convictions and his readiness to support the best program for world government. His criticism of the Americans was not ideological, but was based on his growing conviction that they were not prepared to make the compromises necessary for a stable world. They interpreted every communist act of statesmanship, such as Khrushchev's willingness to remove Soviet missiles from Cuba in the crisis of 1963, as an act of weakness.

Russell's growing association with the youth of the New Left was based on the fact that they, like him, were deeply concerned about the menace of nuclear war. As the New Left's brand of radicalism began to crystallize, their program of social reconstruction, insofar as they had one, resembled Russell's position during World War I. The warnings against the power of scientific bureaucracy, the slogans calling for liberation from institutionalization and the call for a decentralized society, were themes to be found in much of Russell's writing. There can be little doubt that he was far more at home in the radicalism of the sixties that he had been

71

in the Marxist radicalism of the late thirties.

All the activities of his later years are in harmony both with Russell's political philosophy and the program that he had annunciated for years. But in the last five years of Russell's life he underwent a mysterious and fundamental change. He became a supporter of nationalism.

Clearly one of the sentiments Russell held from the first moment he had entered politics was that nationalism was evil. As early as 1901, in the correspondence with Elie Halevy,[119] he proclaimed himself an internationalist. Over the years, Russell's hostility to nationalism grew in intensity to the point where he refused to draw the line between legitimate nationalism of the oppressed and the aggressive nationalism of the imperialists. Even the nationalism of socialist countries was suspect. Russell's sympathy for the underdog never included sympathy for nationalism. As late as October, 1965, in an interview with Enrique Raab, Russell expressed a belief that nationalism was synonymous with the most destructive fanaticism. "I have said this on previous occasions: in 1782, the North American patriot Patrick Henry coined the phrase which gave free rein to all nationalism. He said 'Death before dependence on the British crown.' That is where the disaster started."[120]

Suddenly, six months later, Russell was supporting wars of national liberation. He recalled that "Give me liberty or give me death" was the slogan of the Vietnamese people. Russell was ready to vilify the Soviet position on peaceful coexistence. He wrote:

> If the Soviet Union in its desire for peace, which is commendable, seeks to gain favor with the United States by minimizing or even opposing the struggle for national liberation and socialism, neither peace nor justice will be achieved.[121]

Russell never explained this telling change of emphasis. There were now good nationalisms. This possibility altered all that he had written on the subject.

Russell's reversal of his position on nationalism in *War*

Crimes in Vietnam was sudden, dramatic and above all un-explained. It does seem clear that by 1965 he had become disillusioned with the possibilities for a world government. In the interview with Raab, he stated that he had become dis-illusioned with the possibility of the kind of world government that he had proposed so often. In criticizing the U.N. he said, "It would be necessary to suppress the veto, decree that all national armies must be obliged to participate in a supernational army, etc. And this would not only be used in cases of grave internal conflicts. Can you imagine a group of American soldiers patrolling around some rebel kolkhoz? Or a group of Chinese soldiers putting things in order at Little Rock.... That is why I see the possibilities of a world government in decline. When I wrote *Has Man a Future?* in 1961, I was still convinced; now I am skeptical."[122] It was a few months after this that Russell began to support wars of national liberation.

This scepticism regarding the prospects for a world government is of greatest importance. Russell saw world government as almost a precondition for his program of guild socialism or any other solution to mankind's most urgent problems. His conversion to support of nationalism implied that he had abandoned his earlier hopes for a stable globe brought about through world government. The defence of wars of national liberation and the strident tone of many of his public statements in the closing years of his life imply the end of the scenario for global guild socialism. Perhaps the universal violence that gripped human affairs in the late sixties had driven Russell to supporting nationalism as the only alternative to succumbing to "the crime of silence."

In the course of this essay I have not decisively answered the question of whether there is a political philosophy of Bertrand Russell. It should be clear from this sketch that I believe that there is. It is admittedly peculiar, a revolutionary version of John Stuart Mill. When all the abstract principles are put together and suitably classified the results could be called Whig Socialism.

When Russell is described as an empiricist rather than an

ideologist in politics, one understands by this someone who addresses himself to each problem as it arises, without reference to any fixed philosophical principles. This is certainly not true of Russell. Philosophy has too prominent a place in his political writing. Even those articles that would pass as "letters of advice to the lovelorn" have as one of their consistent themes the idea that people should adopt the right philosophy. Russell's best selling treatises, *The Conquest of Happiness* and *Marriage and Morals*, are rebuttals of the inadequate philosophies that give rise to unhappiness or sexual repression. Few writers consider philosophy, at least bad philosophy, so crucial to human affairs. Russell's *History of Western Philosophy* is almost Hegelian in its insistence that philosophy is a crucial element in the history of the world. In the book Fascism is derived from the epistemology of Fichte and the ontology of Hegel and modern unhappiness is traced to the principles of Lord Byron. One could deduce the Vietnam War from his account of John Dewey. Philosophy certainly acts in the world. Beyond this, there are ethical principles clearly present in all of Russell's work, principles such as the refusal to speak of society as more or other than the aggregate of the individuals in it.

Russell was clearly preoccupied with the problem of individual freedom in the mechanized age. He has often been dismissed as an old fashioned individualist whose writings contain no conception of "social man." This is certainly true but what gives a certain poignance to his struggles is that he was aware of the fact that the individualism of his ancestors was no longer appropriate. Russell insisted that we need a "social concept," but, having stated this, he could not go beyond rather murky Benthamite formulae (such as those that are to be found in *Human Society in Ethics and Politics*) or some vague preaching about how individuals should divest themselves of their aggressive impulses. At the same time in *Conquest of Happiness* Rusell writes of the necessity for every individual to have an enduring link with community. But again he fails to provide a conception of community solid enough for the individual to know what he or she is linked to. In this study I have not attempted to outline a conception of "social man," rather I have tried to show the two sides of Russell: the libertarian which emerges when he addresses individuals, and the technocratic when he addresses mass man. The tension between these two sides as they appear in Russell's writing, is a tension that helps define contemporary liberal civilization, just as the tension between the church of Rome and the ever present heresies helps define Mediaeval Christianity. Russell's place within this liberal tradition is as a stormy meeting point of all the discords in the liberal cosmos.

NOTES

[1]Noam Chomsky, *Problems of Knowledge and Freedom* (London: Barrie & Jenkins, 1971).

[2]David Horowitz, "Bertrand Russell — The Final Passion," *Ramparts,* vol. 8, April 1970. Horowitz calls attention to the fact that Russell supported the revolution, but not its methods.

[3]See Richard Crossman, *The God That Failed* (London: Hamish Hamilton, 1950).

In this work, a series of essays by penitent Communists on how they were misled by Marxism, Russell is praised as one of the "few men" who saw through Communism. "Bertrand Russell has been able to republish his *Practice and Theory of Bolshevism*, written in 1920, without altering a single comma; but most of those who are now so wise and contemptuous after the event were . . . blind." (p. 9)

[4]Bertrand Russell, *New Hopes for a Changing World* (London: Allen & Unwin,1951), pp. 32-41.

[5]Bertrand Russell, *Icarus* (New York: E.P. Dutton & Co., 1924).

[6]Sidney Hook, "Bertrand Russell the Man," *Commentary* July 1976, p. 54.

[7]Ken Coates, "The Internationalism of Bertrand Russell," *Essays in Socialist Humanism*, ed. Ken Coates (Spokesman Books, 1972).

[8]*The Archives of Bertrand Russell*, ed. Barry Feinberg (London: Continuum I Ltd., 1967), p. 7.

[9]Michael Ross, "The Mythology of Friendship: D.H. Lawrence, Bertrand Russell, and 'The Blind Man'," *English Literature and British Philosophy*, ed. S.P. Rosenbaum (Univ. of Chicago Press, 1971), pp. 285-316.

[10]*The Autobiography of Bertrand Russell*, vol. III (New York: Simon & Schuster, 1969), p. 329.

[11]"Reply to Criticisms" in P.A. Schilpp, *The Philosophy of Bertrand Russell* (Evanston, Northwestern Univ. Press, 1944), p. 730.

[12]Bertrand Russell, *Principles of Social Reconstruction* (London: Allen & Unwin, 1916), p. 9.

[13]*Power* (New York: Norton, 1938), p. 12.

[14]Amongst Russell's autobiographical writings are the three volume *Autobiography,* 1967-69 *My Philosophical Development* (1959), *Portraits from Memory* (1956).

[15]This is described in detail in R. Rempel "Russell's First Crusade" (forthcoming).

[16]For a detailed account of Russell's activities in the Peace Movement see J. Newberry, *Bertrand Russell and the Pacifists in the First World War*, Ph.D. thesis, McMaster University, 1975. (forthcoming, Harvester Press).

[17]Bertrand Russell, *Unpopular Essays* (London: Allen & Unwin, 1950), p. 27.

[18]H. Parris, "The Political Thought of Bertrand Russell," *Durham University Journal*, vol. 28, 1965, pp. 86-94. For a persuasive argument against treating Russell as a political philosopher see J. Slater, "The Political Philosophy of Bertrand Russell," *Russell in Review*, ed. J.E. Thomas and K. Blackwell (Toronto: Samuel Stevens Hakkert & Co., 1976), pp. 135-137.

[19]Bertrand Russell, *The Practice and Theory of Bolshevism* (London: Allen & Unwin, 1920), p. 64 (of new edition, 1962).

[20]Bertrand Russell, *Authority and the Individual* (London: Allen & Unwin, 1949), p. 15.

[21]Parris, op. cit., p. 91.

[22]Katharine Tait, *My Father Bertrand Russell* (London: Gollancz, 1976). This is certainly one of the best books on Russell and gives a frank but loving account of the conflicts discussed in this essay.

[23]He once called Prime Minister Macmillan and President Kennedy "The wickedest men who ever lived." His accounts of the Philosophies of Kant and Hegel in the *History of Western Philosophy* (1945) also fall into the category of caricatures.

[24]John Maynard Keynes, *Two Memoirs* (London: Rupert Hart-Davis, 1949), p. 102.

[25]R. Jager, *The Development of Bertrand Russell's Philosophy* (London: Allen & Unwin, 1972).

[26]M. Cranston, "Bertrand Russell," *Encounter*, April 1976, pp. 65-79.

[27]Tait, op. cit.

[28]Ibid., p. 184.

[29]Bertrand Russell, *Autobiography*, vol. I (McClelland & Stewart, 1967), p. 146.

[30]Ibid., vol. II, p. 18.

[31]Tait, op. cit., p. 184.

[32]Bertrand Russell, *Principles of Social Reconstruction* pp. 246-7.

[33]Before World War I Russell's popular writings about science refer to the bleak world that science depicts. During World War I he turns to the theme of the dangerous world that it has created.

[34]Bertrand Russell, *Power*, p. 31.

[35]Ibid., p. 32.

[36]For a summary of these developments see G. Barraclough, *Introduction to Contemporary History* (Modern Thinkers Library, 1965).

[37]Russell to Murray, Sept. 26, 1903, unpublished correspondence.

[38]Bertrand Russell, *Freedom vs. Organization 1814-1914* (New York: Norton, 1934), p. 121.

[39]This story is told in Kinglsey Martin, *Editor* (London: Hutchinson of London, 1968), pp. 193-196.

[40]"International Government," *New Commonwealth*, 9 (Jan. 1948), p. 80.

[41]See report in *United Empire*, Jan.-Feb. 1948, p. 19.

[42]Ibid., p. 22.

[43]Bertrand Russell and Dora Russell, *The Prospects of Industrial Civilization* (London: Allen & Unwin, 1923), pp. 89-90.

[44]*New Hopes*, p. 77.

[45]Karl Marx, *Grundrisse* (Penguin Books).

[46]To say that Russell was in the camp of the New Left does not mean that he was an advocate of drug-taking or many of the other expressions of the New Left culture. But the broad similarities, the mixtures of "participatory democracy," etc., between Russell's political aspirations and those of the New Left suggest the possibility that the New Left and phenomena like it are expressions of a radicalized liberalism.

[47]*Autobiography*, vol. II (Toronto: McClelland & Stewart, 1968), p. 39.

[48]Bertrand Russell, *Unpopular Essays* (London: Allen & Unwin, 1950), p. 223.

[49]See Arnold Toynbee, "The Unity of Gilbert Murray's Life and Work," *Gilbert Murray an Unfinished Biography*, ed. Jean Smith and Arnold Toynbee (London: Allen & Unwin, 1961), p. 215.

[50]B. Russell to G. Murray, Dec. 12, 1902. Russell Archives, McMaster University.

[51]B. Russell to G. Murray, April 9, 1943.

[52]*Freedom vs. Organization*, p. 72.

[53]Ibid., p. 73.

[54]Ibid., p. 100.

[55]Ibid., p. 121.

[56]Bertrand Russell, *The Problem of China* (New York: Century, 1922), pp. 208-209.

[57]*Autobiography*, vol. II, p. 16.

[58]Bertrand Russell, "The Ancestry of Fascism," *In Praise of Idleness* (London: Allen & Unwin, 1935), p. 67.

[59]Bertrand Russell, *Political Ideals* (New York: The Century Co., 1917), p. 19.

[60]Ibid., p. 27.

[61]Richard Wollheim, "Bertrand Russell and the Liberal Tradition," in *Bertrand Russell's Philosophy*, ed. George Nakhnikian (London: Duckworth, 1974), pp. 209-221.

[62]"Two Statements on Invasion of Czechoslovakia," *London Bulletin*, no. 6, Autumn, 1968, p. 84.

[63]B. Russell to Clifford Allen, Feb. 2, 1918. Bertrand Russell Archives, McMaster University.

[64]"Philosophy and Politics," *Unpopular Essays*. Russell's assessment of Hegel in this and other essays is outrageous; e.g. "It follows from his [Hegel's] metaphysic that true liberty consists in obedience to an arbitrary authority," p. 22. This assessment is one of the instances where the "empiricist temper" shows itself to be a form of dogmatism.

[65]G.D.H. Cole to Russell, Sept. 28, 1917. Bertrand Russell Archives, McMaster University.

[66]*Political Ideals*, p. 34.

[67]*Prospects*, p. 57.

[68]*Political Ideals*, p. 16.

[69]To demonstrate this point one would have to collect all of Russell's statements on collectivity in the modern era and analyze them. I suspect that theory such as the one I indicate, collectivities formed by industrialism are made, would emerge. The occurrence of the term lunatic in many of Russell's political writings following World War I strongly suggests this.

[70]*Autobiography*, vol. I, p. 104.

[71]G.D.H. Cole to Russell. Sept. 28, 1917.

[72]Ken Coates, "The Internationalism of Bertrand Russell," *Essays on Socialist Humanism* (Nottingham: Spokesman Books, 1972), p. 207.

[73]Bertrand Russell, *A History of Western Philosophy* (London: Allen & Unwin, 1946), p. 783.
   American pragmatism is included among the power philosophies discussed in *Power*.

[74]Ibid.

[75]Bertrand Russell, "Science as an Element in Culture," *New Statesman*, Lon. (24-31 May 1913), 202-4, 234-6. Reprinted as "The Place of Science in a Liberal Education," in *Mysticism and Logic* (New York, Norton, 1929), p. 33

[76]Bertrand Russell, *Wisdom of the West*, ed. Paul Foulkes, (New York: Crescent Press, 1964), p. 311.

[77]Bertrand Russell, *The Scientific Outlook* (New York: Norton, 1931), p. 140.

[78]Ibid.

[79]Bertrand Russell, "Citizenship in a Great State," *Fortune*, Dec. 1943.

[80]"State Socialism," Bertrand Russell, Unpublished Essays 1889, Bertrand Russell Archives, McMaster University.

[81]Ibid.

[82]Ibid.

[83]Ibid.

[84]Ibid.

[85]Ibid.

[86]"Evolution as affecting Modern Political Science," B. Russell, Unpublished Essays 1889. Bertrand Russell Archives, McMaster University.

[87]Ibid.

[88]At various stages of his life he claimed that he detested communism and capitalism equally. Russell's views on Marxism require a more comprehensive treatment, for most writings on the subject use Russell as an arsenal of anti-Marxist arguments. In spite of his many criticisms, he was sympathetic on many vital points. In *Power*, a book composed in the 1930's, he cites pragmatism as a power philosophy, but not Marxism.

[89]Bertrand Russell, *German Social Democracy* (London: Longmans, Green, 1896), p. 6.

[90]Ibid., p. 7.

[91]Ibid., p. 36.

[92]Ibid., p. 171.

[93]Ibid., p. 164.

[94]Russell to Murray, Sept. 9, 1903.

[95]"An Open Letter to President Wilson," *The Survey*, vol. 37, 30 Dec. 1916, 372-73, also *Autobiography* vol. II, pp. 28-29.

[96]Bertrand Russell, "Socialism and Liberal Ideals," *Living Age*, July, 1920, p. 118.

[97]Bertrand Russell, *Sceptical Essays* (London: Allen & Unwin, 1928).

[98]Bertrand Russell, "Communism by Stages," *Daily Herald*, July 5, 1927.

[99]Bertrand Russell, *Practice and Theory of Bolshevism*, p. 7.

[100]Ibid., p. 75.

[101]Ibid.,

[102]*Prospects*, p. 25.

[103]*Social Reconstruction*, p. 110.

[104]*Sceptical Essays*, p. 23.

[105]Bertrand Russell, "The Effect of Science on Social Institutions," *Survey* (April 1924), reprinted in *Sceptical Essays*.

[106]"Outline of a Political Philosophy," unpublished manuscript prepared as series of

lectures in America during World War II. Bertrand Russell Archives, McMaster University.

[107]*Unpopular Essays*, p. 55.

[108]"The Duty of a Philosopher in This Age." Bertrand Russell in *The Abdication of Philosophy: Philosophy and the Public Good*, ed. Eugene Freeman (LaSalle, Illinois: Open Court 1976).

[109]*History of Western Philosophy*, pp. 556-557.

[110]*Scientific Outlook*, p. 217.

[111]Ibid.

[112]Ibid.

[113]Bertrand Russell, *Authority and the Individual* (London: 1949), p. 1.

[114]C.L. Sulzberger, "A Corpse on Horseback," *New York Times*, May 12, 1967, sec. iv, p. 46.

[115]"Congress of Cultural Freedom (File)" Russell to American Com. for Cultural Freedom, May 16, 1953. Bertrand Russell Archives, McMaster University.

[116]Ibid., Russell to Stephen Spender, April 14, 1956.

[117]Russell makes this same point in a letter reprinted in a charming collection, *Dear Bertrand Russell*, ed. Barry Feinburg and Ronald Kasrils (Boston: Houghton Mifflin Co., 1969), p. 119-120.

[118]*Autobiography*, vol. III, p. 474.

[119]There is a long and interesting correspondence with Halévy in the Bertrand Russel Archives during the Free Trade vs. Protectionism dispute of the first decade of the twentieth century.

[120]Interview with Enrique Raab, *Sunday Citizen*, Oct. 31, 1965.

[121]Bertrand Russell, *War Crimes in Vietnam* (London: Allen & Unwin, 1967), p. 122.
   The change in emphasis occurs with reference to Russell's support for "national liberation" not for his support for the underdog. Russell would have always supported the Vietnamese as an oppressed people without explicitly supporting "national liberation." This shift is very ably discussed by N. Griffin in "Russell's Later Political Thought," *Russell, the Journal of the Russell Archives*, 5, Spring 1972.

[122]Raab, op. cit.